Lynda Field is a trained counsellor and psychotherapist who specializes in personal and group development. She is the author of nine titles, including the bestselling *60 Ways to Feel Amazing*, and *60 Ways to Change Your Life*. In addition to giving seminars and workshops, she writes a column for a major internet provider, as well as articles for a variety of national magazines. She lives in Essex, UK.

Visit Lynda online at www.lyndafield.com

By the same author

60 Ways to Change Your Life
60 Ways to Feel Amazing
The Little Book of Woman Power
60 Tips for Self-Esteem
Creating Self-Esteem
60 Ways to Heal Your Life
More Than 60 Ways to Make Your Life Amazing

The Self-Esteem Workbook

An Interactive Approach to Changing Your Life

Lynda Field

VERMILION
LONDON

1 3 5 7 9 10 8 6 4 2

First published in 1995 by Element Books.
This edition published in 2001 by Vermilion,
an imprint of Ebury Press, Random House,
20 Vauxhall Bridge Road, London SW1V 2SA
www.randomhouse.co.uk

Random House Australia (Pty) Limited
20 Alfred Street, Milsons Point,
Sydney, New South Wales 2061, Australia

Random House New Zealand Limited
18 Poland Road, Glenfield,
Auckland 10, New Zealand

Random House (Pty) Limited
Endulini, 5A Jubilee Road,
Parktown 2193, South Africa

The Random House Group Limited Reg. No. 954009

Papers used by Vermilion are natural, recyclable products made
from wood grown in sustainable forests.

Printed and bound the UK by Biddles of Guildford

A CIP catalogue record for this book
are available from the British Library

ISBN 0-09-185733-3

For Richard

ACKNOWLEDGEMENTS

The inspiration for this book has come from many different sources. In particular I would like to thank all my readers, clients and workshop participants. In sharing their difficulties and triumphs they have helped me to develop a deeper understanding of the importance of self-esteem and of the crucial part that it plays in our lives.

My husband Richard and children Leilah, Jack and Alex have, as always, been a constant strength and support and have shown amazing tolerance, particularly in the last stages of writing whilst I was working to meet the deadline.

Thank you to my mother and father, Barbara and Idwal Goronwy, for being wonderful parents who have always encouraged me.

To Mary Field, my mother-in-law, who is always there when I need her and to Barbara Higham who has helped me in more ways than can be imagined – thank you.

CONTENTS

PREFACE

Your life is a precious gift, miraculous and amazing, but you will not always be able to appreciate this miracle fully.

Our challenges can sometimes be hard to bear. When we face difficulties and defeats we can easily lose our self-belief and our sense of self-worth, and as soon as we stop believing in ourselves the world can become a dull and lonely place.

My first book, *Creating Self-Esteem* was designed to help people understand how to regain their sense of self-respect, self-worth and self-belief. In response to numerous requests for more specialized guidance I have written *The Self-Esteem Workbook*, which develops a new, personalized approach to the creation of self-esteem. This book shows you how to construct a self-esteem action plan to meet your own specific needs.

As you increase your self-esteem and you learn to value and respect yourself, the quality of your life will be enhanced and enriched. To be able to appreciate your life you must first be able to appreciate yourself.

INTRODUCTION

You and Your Self-Esteem

You are unique. There has never been and never will be anyone on Earth who is just like you. You are a special, worthy and lovable person – but sometimes you may find this hard to believe.

Because we are human we are always in the process of learning about ourselves and our world and so we are inevitably facing new challenges all the time. Our biggest challenge will always be *to remember that we are special, worthy and lovable,* however difficult our life may seem to be sometimes. Our self-esteem is a sensitive commodity; our feelings about ourselves can change dramatically from day to day, indeed from moment to moment. Look at the checklist below.

Initial Self-Esteem Checklist

	yes	no
I am optimistic.	____	____
I trust my intuition.	____	____
I believe in myself.	____	____
The world is a beautiful place.	____	____
I express my feelings easily.	____	____
It's OK to be angry.	____	____
I can allow myself to feel sad.	____	____
I am good at making decisions.	____	____
I can say 'no' when I want to.	____	____
It's OK for me to make mistakes.	____	____
I deserve the best that life has to offer.	____	____

How did you answer these questions? Are you feeling powerful, confident, decisive and at one with your world or are you feeling threatened, out of control and insecure? In other words, are you feeling high or low in self-esteem?

What is Self-Esteem?

Listed below are some of the things which people have associated with having high and low self-esteem.

High Self-Esteem	**Low Self-Esteem**
Having confidence	Lacking confidence
Being happy	Being unhappy
Wholeness	A feeling of not belonging
A feeling of being in control	Being out of control
Thinking positively	Thinking negatively
Being in charge	Disempowered
Assertive behaviour	Being a victim
Having self-respect	Having no self-respect
Vitality	Depression
Being at ease	Feeling uptight
Dynamism	No energy
Dignity	Shame
Feeling balanced	Shaky
Being successful	Being a failure
Charismatic personality	Weak personality
Feeling valuable	Feeling unworthy
Being decisive	Being indecisive
Security	Insecurity

How do you relate to these ideas? Do you disagree with any? Have you anything that you would like to add to these lists?

Everybody knows what is meant by the word self-esteem but interestingly this meaning is different for everyone. Self-esteem cannot be defined easily because it is a personal quality. There is however one factor which all agree on: self-esteem makes you feel good. Self-esteem could be described as the 'Feel Good Factor which is based on self-belief'. There is no doubt that when we are high in self-esteem we are feeling good about ourselves and when we are low in self-esteem we feel terrible. Everyone wants to feel good – everyone is looking for self-esteem.

The Self-Esteem Workbook has been designed to provide a practical framework of techniques and activities which will enable you to experience high self-esteem in any aspect of your life. Using the workbook is an interactive experience. When you take part in the activities you will personalize the book. However, it is important to realize that you will only benefit from this experience if you are able to be really honest with your answers. Please don't just say what you think you 'ought' to say: this will not work. If you need help you could discuss difficult exercises with a trusted friend. If you don't know how to answer then leave a blank and come back to that question another time.

When you use the workbook like this it will become a meaningful reflection of your beliefs about yourself. It will provide a personal record of your present levels of self-esteem and it will demonstrate easy-to-use, practical techniques which you can apply to make changes in all areas of your life. You will be able to create new levels of self-esteem in personal relationships and learn to increase your prosperity. Make your life a success! Bring your dreams into reality. Fill your life with self-esteem and enjoy your full potential by discovering your own incredible and unique creativity.

The workbook is divided into two sections. 'Part 1: A Personal Assessment of Your Present Levels of Self-Esteem' shows how you can *choose* to create high or low self-esteem. It examines the personal elements which you bring to each of your life experiences by focusing on your own individual thought, feeling and behaviour patterns. It asks:

What do you think?
How do you feel?
How do you behave?

'Part 2: New Levels of Self-Esteem' demonstrates the practical application of original and easy-to-use techniques to increase your self-esteem in any area of your life. It looks in detail at developing high levels of personal self-esteem, particularly in the following areas:

Trusting yourself
Developing your spirituality
Increasing self-awareness
Improving personal relationships
Increasing prosperity and wealth
Healing your life
Discovering your life's work

The Self-Esteem Workbook is all about you and it is all about change. This book will change you and often it is difficult to accept change. Sometimes we make amazing leaps forward in our lives and forget how far we have come and how much effort it took us to progress. Be kind with yourself. If you find yourself continually moving the goalposts, *stop* and acknowledge your achievements. The biggest inner changes are always linked with an increased capacity for self-respect, self-love and self-esteem. Respect the way you approach your difficulties. Admire the fact that you bought this book and that you are prepared to change. Every time you give yourself encouragement you are increasing your self-esteem. If you find that a particular topic in the book is too sensitive an issue for you then leave it for another time and move on to a different section – what is hard one day may be easy the next.

You can use this book in many ways. You may want to read it all the way through and then go back and do the exercises. On the other hand you may be moved to dip in and out as the fancy takes you. Use this book in whichever way works best for you.

Remember that, as we change our old patterns, as we stop operating in the old mode but haven't quite got used to the new ways of thinking, feeling and behaving, we will sometimes experience a feeling of confusion. If this happens *hang on in there*; know that this is just a short period of transition. Admire your tenacity, respect your creativity, love your strength of purpose.

I hope that this book will become a powerful resource for you. *You deserve all love and support on your quest for self-esteem.*

PART 1

A Personal Assessment of Your Present Levels of Self-Esteem

1

High or Low Self-Esteem – The Choice is Yours

Self-belief is the cornerstone of self-esteem. If I believe that I am worthless, no good and incapable, then my *feelings* about myself will reflect these *thoughts*. My *behaviour* will reflect my low self-opinion and so my whole experience will be one of low self-esteem. When we criticize and blame ourselves our *behaviour* will always be ineffective.

If, however, my *thoughts* about myself are supporting and validating and I believe that I am intrinsically a worthy person who deserves self-respect, then my *feelings* about myself will be correspondingly positive. And so my *behaviour* will be creative and effective – I will be able to make things happen in my life. Our self-belief, or *thoughts* about ourselves, directly affect our *feelings* and our *behaviour*.

How Do You Think, Feel and Behave?

To every experience we bring our whole self, we integrate our mind, body, spirit and emotions. This means that our *thoughts, feelings* and *behaviour* exist simultaneously and that they are interrelated; they affect each other and in fact create each other. See Figure 1.

Figure 1
A whole experience

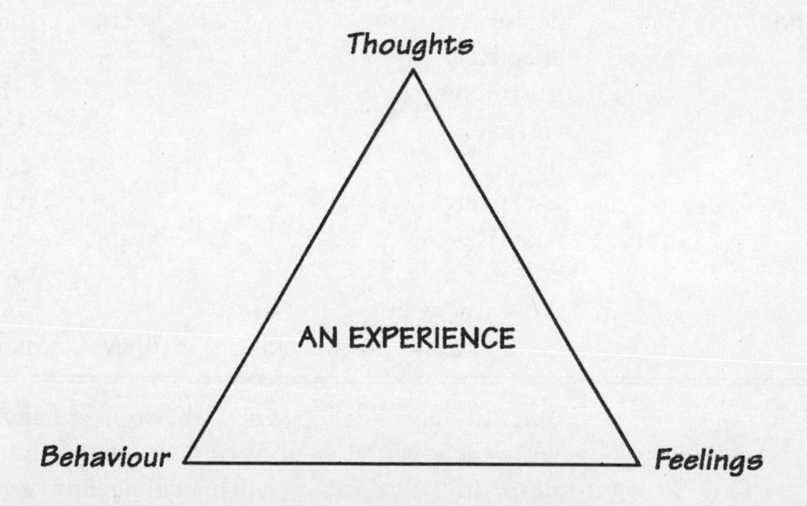

Every experience is a culmination of our thoughts, feelings and behaviour. The *quality* of the experience depends entirely upon the nature of the thoughts and feelings we have and the ways in which we behave. The following table demonstrates the different thoughts, feelings and behaviour which together create the experiences of high and low self-esteem.

		High Self-Esteem		Low Self-Esteem
Thinks	I . . .	believe in myself	I . . .	don't believe in myself
		trust my intuition		am not deserving
		deserve the best		have no self-respect
		am worthy		am a victim
		respect myself		am powerless
		respect others		am a failure
		can make things happen		am no good
		can change		can't change
		am a success		am too ________
		do the best I can		am not good enough
Feels	I am . . .	spontaneous	I am . . .	uptight
		free		insecure
		caring		antisocial
		optimistic		depressed
		appreciative		guilty
		balanced		worried
		positive		critical
		in touch with my emotions		afraid of my emotions
		secure		victimized
Behaves	I act . . .	decisively	I act . . .	indecisively
		effectively		fearfully
		trustingly		critically
		creatively		judgementally
		openly		defensively
		assertively		passively/aggressively
	I can . . .	take risks	I can't . . .	take risks
		say 'no'		say 'no'
		show my feelings		show my feelings
	I have . . .	good communication skills	I have . . .	poor communication skills

Our thoughts, feelings and behaviour are always changing. Our levels of self-esteem can alter from one minute to the next. You may be swinging along full of positive self-beliefs, feeling great and then. . . something happens. This 'something' can be any circumstance which knocks you off balance by encouraging self-criticism. And so, the thoughts which were supporting your high self-esteem change. You suddenly sink into the whirlpool of your negative self-beliefs. Instead of believing that you deserve the best and that you can 'make things happen', you are now believing that you are worthless and hence powerless to change anything – you have become a victim of circumstances! The speed at which this change can happen is really quite frightening. As soon as the quality of your thoughts changes, your feelings and behaviour correspond. Instead of feeling optimistic, positive and caring, you are now insecure, critical and negative. Your behaviour will exactly match your thoughts and feelings and so now instead of acting decisively and creatively, you will be fearful and ineffective.

EXERCISE When High Self-Esteem Changes to Low Self-Esteem

Think of a time when you felt high in self-esteem and then something occurred which totally demoralized you. Perhaps someone criticized you in a particularly sensitive area, or maybe you felt that you were shown up in some way.

1 Describe how you thought about yourself when you were high in self-esteem, *before* the event occurred.

____

____

____

____

2 How did you feel at this time?

____

____

____

____

3 How did you act, before the event?

____

____

____

____

Try to reconstruct the exact circumstances surrounding this situation. Recreate the sensations which were linked with losing your self-esteem.

4 What were your thoughts about yourself *after* the event?

5 What feelings do you associate with your loss of self-esteem at this time?

6 How did your behaviour change after the event had occurred?

It seems as if our self-esteem is always on the line. We can go up and down and up and down again with alarming speed. Does this sound like you? Take heart: all of us are always working on our self-esteem – we have to because we did not learn to believe in our intrinsic worthiness when we were children and so we need to learn it now. Our self-esteem is rather like a beautiful but delicate flower and it needs constant nourishment and care in order for it to grow and remain protected.

Maintaining Our Self-Esteem

The nurturing of our self-esteem requires that we are continually doing maintenance work on ourselves. We have seen how our thoughts, feelings and behaviour come together to create our experiences. If our thoughts change then this affects our feelings and our subsequent behaviour. Similarly, if our feelings alter then our thoughts and behaviour will change. If we change our behaviour this will have an immediate effect upon our thoughts and feelings. The interdependency of our thoughts, feelings and behaviour means that if we *consciously change* any one of these three we can transform the nature of our experience. Let's see how this works.

EXERCISE

The Cycle of Change

Review your answers to the previous exercise. Notice the particular relationship between your thoughts, feelings and behaviour before and then after the situation which swept you from high to low self-esteem. It is possible to change the effects of this process – we can retrieve our self-esteem! Figure 2 (page 14), 'The cycle of change', shows how we can do this.

Take your answers to questions 4, 5 and 6 and insert them in the appropriate places in Figure 2(a). Describe the demoralizing event in the space provided. Now look at your completed Figure 2(a).

What does it show you about the relationship between your thoughts, feelings and behaviour?

Do these elements have a knock-on effect?

Do they seem to create each other?

Look at the answers you have inserted in the figure. Which, if any, of those reactions could you change?

Could you change your thoughts about the situation? For example, would you have been so crushed if you had been able to maintain a strong belief in yourself, regardless of the circumstances?

Could you change your feelings surrounding the event? For example, would it have been possible to bring some humour into the situation, perhaps that might have lightened the load?

Would it be possible to act differently? Perhaps you didn't say what you would have liked to have said or maybe you said too much.

Reflect on the event, thoughts, feelings and actions which cost you your self-esteem. There is always so much scope for us to change, unless we want to be stuck for some reason. The change cycle is a useful tool for helping to understand our reactions to circumstances and to see how we could cope differently and maintain our self-esteem.

Think of one reaction which you could change. Insert this in the appropriate place in Figure 2(b).

2(a)

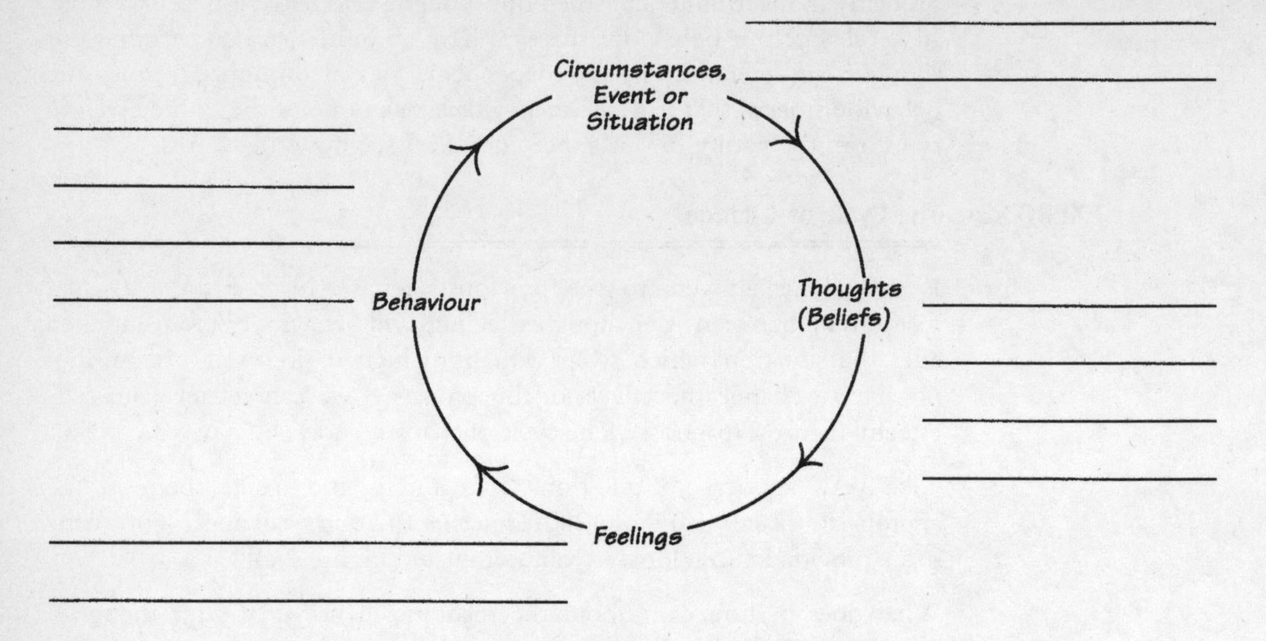

2(b)

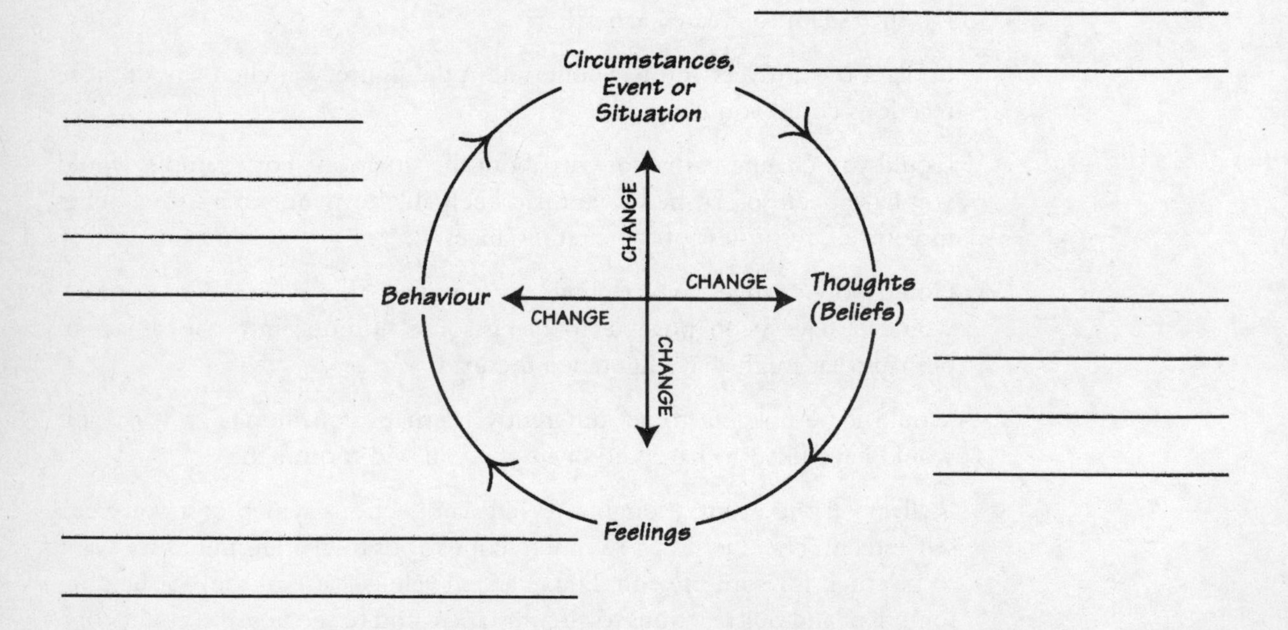

Figure 2 The cycle of change

How does this change the other elements in Figure 2(b)?

____

____

____

____

Now you have changed one response in the diagram, fill in the other spaces. Has everything changed? Has this response changed the initial circumstances? Be as creative as you can. Feel free to use your imagination to create a completely different scenario.

Next time a similar situation arises could you maintain your self-esteem?

Draw your own change cycles and use them when you are looking low self-esteem in the eye. Be creative: remember you can always change. If your reactions can create low self-esteem then they can also create high self-esteem. Choose reactions which support your self-esteem.

2
What Do You Think?

A man is largely what he thinks about all day long.
Ralph Waldo Emerson

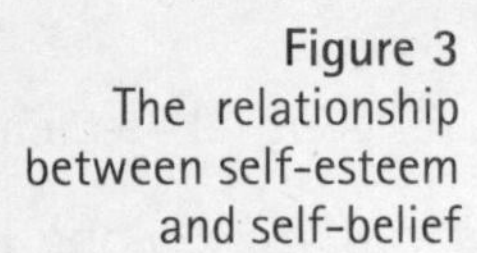
Figure 3
The relationship between self-esteem and self-belief

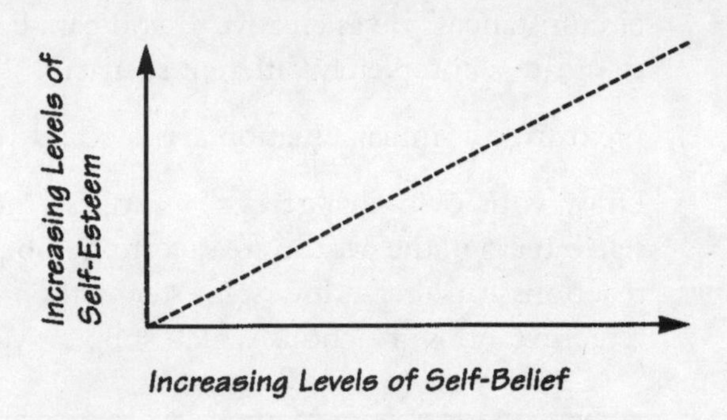

Our self-esteem rises and falls in direct proportion to our self-belief (Figure 3), so any discussion of self-esteem must involve our self-beliefs.

EXERCISE Your Self-Image

What do you believe to be true about yourself? Look at the following words. Read through this list putting the words 'I am' before each of them and score as follows:

0 almost never
1 sometimes
2 often
3 almost always

___ tolerant ___ articulate ___ interesting
___ depressed ___ worthless ___ lovable
___ adventurous ___ kind ___ shy
___ bossy ___ negative ___ lazy
___ cynical ___ trustworthy ___ unemotional
___ intelligent ___ supportive ___ amusing

___ irritable ____ worthy ____ joyful

___ self-conscious ____ proud ____ critical

___ free ____ caring ____ predictable

___ stupid ____ self-aware ____ foolish

___ sensitive ____ indecisive ____ happy

___ protective ____ passive ____ optimistic

___ overbearing ____ miserable ____ demanding

___ capable ____ flexible ____ temperamental

___ fearful ____ helpless ____ confident

___ boring ____ sensitive ____ controlled

___ intuitive ____ embarrassed ____ reflective

___ guilty ____ spontaneous ____ rigid

1 Look at where you scored 3. What do you think that you are almost always?

I am almost always:

______________ ______________ ______________

______________ ______________ ______________

______________ ______________ ______________

______________ ______________ ______________

These characteristics are part of your self-image. Now consider the ways in which these features of your personality affect your level of self-esteem.

____

____

____

____

____

____

Which, if any, of these characteristics would you like to change?

2 Now look at where you scored 0. What do you believe that you are almost never?

I am almost never:

Your self-image does not include these features. Think of the ways in which the apparent lack of these qualities affects the level of your self-esteem.

Which, if any, of your 'almost never' characteristics would you like to increase?

3 List six adjectives which you think best describe you; these can be from the above list or not:

I am:

______________ ______________ ______________

______________ ______________ ______________

Choose the statement which you think is most important. This is your core belief about yourself, the personal self-belief which underlies your self-image.

My core belief is that I am:

____

What does your core belief reveal to you? Does this statement criticize you or appreciate you? Does it support low or high self-esteem?

4 Now write down any qualities you have which you like about yourself. Explain why you like these features and how they relate to your level of self-esteem.

____

____

____

____

Please use more paper whenever you need to!

5 List any characteristics which you think would further enhance your self-image.

______________ ______________ ______________

______________ ______________ ______________

______________ ______________ ______________

______________ ______________ ______________

Self-Image Review

By now you will have an idea of

- What sort of person you think you are
- The self-beliefs which enhance your self-esteem
- The self-beliefs which support your low self-esteem
- The qualities you would like to incorporate in your self-image

If I believe that I am lazy, stupid and worthless then my self-esteem will be very low. If I believe that I am interesting, capable and lovable my self-esteem will be high.

Perhaps you are thinking that all this is very obvious – if you feel good about yourself you will be high in self-esteem and if you feel badly about yourself you will have low self-esteem. So what? Someone said to me recently, 'Look I am what I am, nothing can change that. I've never struck lucky in my life and everything I've done has gone wrong. Why should I believe that anything will ever change for me?'

The good news is that we don't have to wait for things to change for us.

We can change the quality of our lives by changing the ways we think about ourselves and our world.

Your Beliefs Can Be Changed

We learned our beliefs about ourselves when we were very young. We came to understand ourselves and our world through interpretation by the most influential adult figures in our lives, usually our parents. We have *learned* our perceptions of our self and the world. As babies and small children we unquestioningly absorbed and believed all the messages which were relayed in our environment. These might have been spoken messages which criticized or appreciated us or they may have been more subtle thought and behaviour patterns which influenced our home life.

As you work through this book you will see how these internalized messages from your childhood can have far-reaching implications for you in all areas of your life. If you have learned beliefs about yourself which don't value and support you then you can change these beliefs. Remember that your self-esteem rises and falls in direct relationship with your self-belief!

EXERCISE Self-Esteem Visualization

1 Find a quiet place and sit comfortably. Take some deep breaths and relax your body. Now; remember a time when you were high in self-esteem – it doesn't matter how long ago this time was. Close your eyes and see yourself in this confident, decisive and relaxed mode. Try to remember the details of the experience. Where were you? Who was with you? What did you feel like? Imagine that you are recreating those exact feelings. You are feeling great. The world is a wonderful place: *what are you believing about yourself?*

____

____

____

____

2 Close your eyes again and now recreate an occasion when you were low in self-esteem. It probably won't be too difficult to remember exactly what it felt like. Feel the painful emotions as clearly as possible and ask yourself: *what do I believe to be true about myself now*?

____

____

____

____

Come back to the present and ask yourself: *which set of beliefs is true*?

If we have different beliefs about ourselves at different times then obviously our beliefs must be changeable. This is a very important realization.

EXERCISE We Are What We Believe We Are

1 Because we think the same thoughts over and over again it is hard to believe that we actually choose our thoughts. Look at these ideas:

I am a wonderful, unique person.
I am creative and aware.
I deserve the very best that life has to offer.

How often do you have thoughts like these? Do you ever have such thoughts or do you refuse to think that such ideas apply to you?

You are a wonderful, creative and aware person. Your qualities are unique and you deserve to experience the best that life can offer.

This affirmation describes you!

Do you believe it or do you think it isn't true?____________________

If you don't believe it, why don't you?

____

____

____

____

2 If we can refuse to accept positive self-beliefs then it must also be possible to refuse to accept negative self-beliefs. Think about the list below:

I'm so:	stupid	I'm too:	fat
	worthless		thin
	useless		lazy
	pathetic		weak

Do you ever speak to yourself like this?

Can you add anything to this list? In what ways do you criticize yourself?

______________ ______________ ______________

______________ ______________ ______________

______________ ______________ ______________

______________ ______________ ______________

When we criticize and blame ourselves we cannot be effective in our lives. If we choose to take on negative self-beliefs then we will always be low in self-esteem.

EXERCISE I Should, I Ought to, I Must

1 Make a list of all the things which you think that you should, ought to or must do.

I should/ought to/must:

____

____

____

____

____

____

Whenever you hear yourself using words such as, 'ought to', 'must', 'supposed to', 'have to' and 'should', just stop for a moment. These words imply that there is a right thing to do and that you are guilty of not having done it yet. Maybe you do need to fulfil an obligation and, if so, the best thing is to get the job done. However, more often than not, these directives are based on someone else's ideas about how we should be running our lives.

I ought to be nicer to __________________________
I should love my father.
I must be more positive.
I have to be more thoughtful.
I shouldn't say what I think.
I ought to like this child.

I have heard hundreds of replies to this exercise. We all seem to have great long lists of things which we can criticize ourselves for not doing.

2 Consider your replies. Take each item, read it out loud and then ask yourself why you should/ought to/must/have to do this particular thing.

EXAMPLE:

Statement: *I should always be nice to people.*

Question: *Why should I always be nice to people?*

Answers: *My mother/teacher said I should.*
Because everybody has to be nice.
So that everyone will like me.
I don't want to rock the boat.

Your answers may surprise you. Our personal list of directives is largely based on a set of irrational beliefs which we have long accepted as being true. Do these beliefs really work for you? Do they increase your positive self-beliefs or do they undermine your feelings of self-worth? Do they support high or low self-esteem? Are they really true for you?

Your Self-Belief and Your Self-Esteem

Positive self-beliefs create high self-esteem and negative self-beliefs create low self-esteem. Figure 4 shows how we can make our own self-fulfilling prophecy. (This diagram first appeared in my book *Creating Self-Esteem*.)

Figure 4
Cycles of self-belief and self-esteem

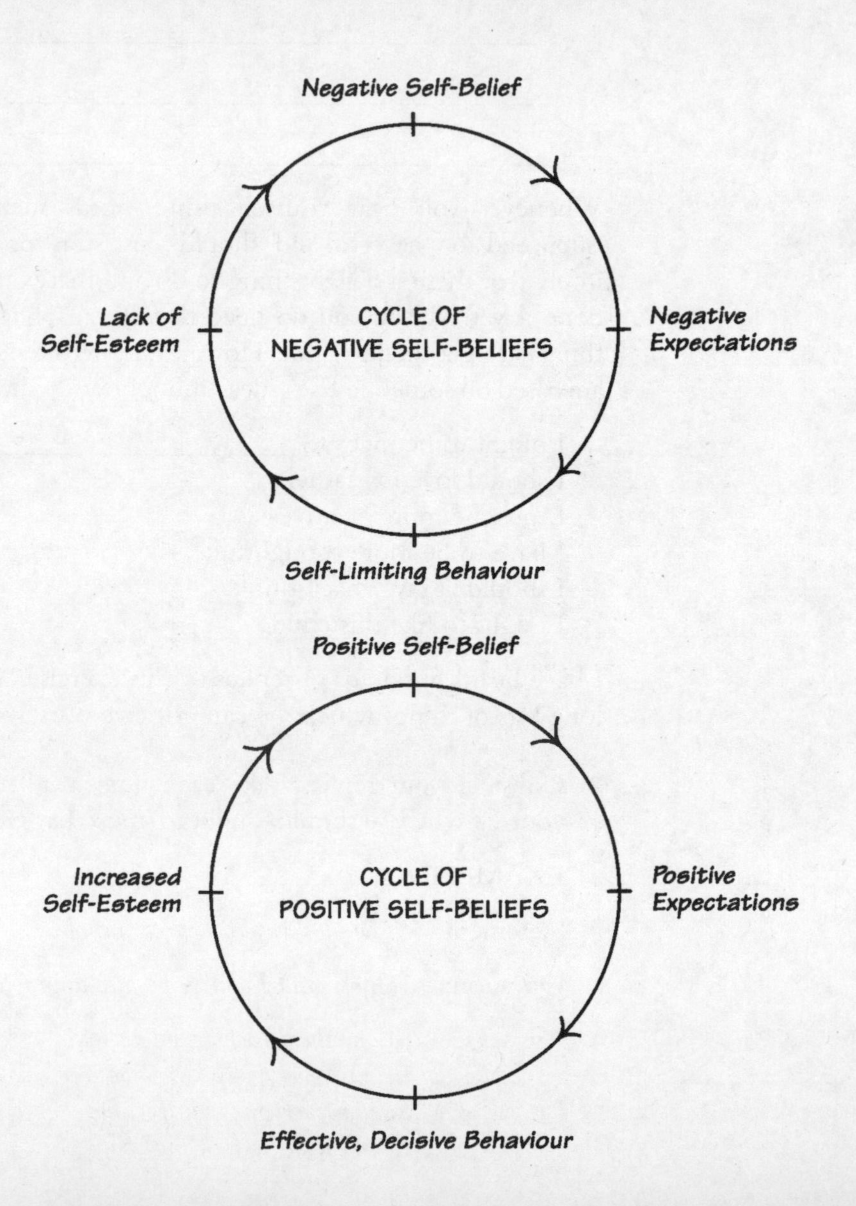

Imagine a day when you wake up feeling wonderful, you are confident, happy and relaxed. When you believe in yourself anything becomes possible. Because you have positive expectations you will be on the look-out for any advantageous situation which may come your way. Your behaviour will be effective and decisive, your self-esteem will increase and so you will reinforce your belief in yourself.

Now, imagine a day when things don't feel so good. You are feeling low and insecure – we all know only too well how this feels! You look out at a world where everything seems to be happening to someone else; everyone has got their life together, except you. You expect the worst to happen and so it does. Even if a wonderful opportunity came your way you would either miss it or feel that you weren't good enough to take advantage of it. Your behaviour is ineffective because you can't make decisions . . . and so the day goes on to prove exactly what you knew to be true. Your self-esteem falls even lower, which reinforces your original self-belief.

EXERCISE Your Positive and Negative Self-Beliefs

1 Think of a time when you were feeling positive about yourself. Relax and close your eyes and try to experience exactly what it felt like. What were your self-beliefs? Try to be as explicit as possible.

I believed that I:

____

____

____

____

2 What did you believe was possible for you? What were your expectations?

I expected that:

____

____

____

____

How did you behave?

____

____

____

____

How did you feel about yourself?

I felt:

____

____

____

____

3 Now think of a time when you were feeling negative about yourself. Ask yourself the same questions. How different are your answers?

____

____

____

____

The Law of Attraction states that we create whatever we think about. We live within an electromagnetic field and each time we think, we charge the energy field with vibrations. Like attracts like and so, whilst negative thought patterns attract all forms of negativity, positive thought patterns attract all forms of positivity.

What sort of thoughts are you thinking all day long? What are you attracting into your life?

When we know how these two belief cycles work we can truly understand that we are what we think we are.

You are an amazing person with unlimited potential and you deserve to be high in self-esteem.

Believe this to be true and self-esteem will be yours.

Summary of the Relationship between Self-Belief and Self-Esteem

1 Self-esteem could be described as the 'Feel Good Factor which is based upon self-belief'.

2 Self-esteem rises and falls in direct proportion to the quality of our self-belief.

3 Your core belief reveals whether you are high or low in self-esteem.

4 You have *learned* your beliefs about yourself and the world. These beliefs can be changed.

5 You are what you believe you are.
You can refuse to accept beliefs which don't support your self-esteem.

6 You are a wonderful, creative and aware human being. Your qualities are unique and you deserve to experience the best that life can offer.
You can *learn* to accept thoughts which increase your self-esteem.

7 Positive self-beliefs create high self-esteem and negative self-beliefs create low self-esteem.

8 Your thoughts are creating your reality. You can choose to think appreciatively or critically about yourself. You can create high or low self-esteem.

3
How Do You Feel?

Would you describe yourself as an emotional or unemotional person?

Some people are acutely sensitive at the emotional level; they are very much in touch with their own feelings and also extremely aware of the feelings of others. If you are like this you will certainly know it because this type of awareness can be difficult to handle. It is so easy to become swamped by emotion, whether it is our own or someone else's. If we become overwhelmed by feelings our thoughts and actions will be immediately affected and our total experience will become limited. Think of a time when you got into a tizz over something. What happened to you mentally? Did you experience any physical sensations? How did you behave?

When we feel at the mercy of our emotions we fall into a state of confusion; our judgement becomes clouded ('Is that the right thing to do?'); we may have physical symptoms (butterflies, anxiety attacks, tension headaches); our behaviour may not be what we expected it to be (perhaps we say 'yes' when we wanted to say 'no', maybe we were too afraid to do what we had planned to do). It is difficult to react rationally when our emotions are in full flood.

Other people appear to be acutely insensitive at the emotional level. Do you know someone who is like this? These people seem to be quite unaffected by the emotional tides of life. The ability to operate rationally is a great gift but not if it is earned at the expense of our emotions. 'Supercool' may mean 'super-insensitive'. If we are not in touch with our own feelings we will be unaware of the feelings of others. If we deny our feelings then we again limit our total experience. Think of a time when you strangled an emotion because you felt that it would be too painful for some reason. What happened to your thoughts? How did you behave?

Super-rational or super-emotional, the price is high; it is the loss of a creative and validating experience and it will cost us our self-esteem. Our self-esteem develops when we can balance our rationality and our emotions. We need both qualities in our lives. Emotional awareness is a quality which helps us to cultivate the imaginative and creative parts of our nature and we shall see how very important it is to develop our sensitivity in these areas. However, in order to express our creativity we need also to be able to exercise our logical and rational abilities.

Super-rationality emerges when we deny our feelings and remain unaware of our imaginative and creative potential. This denial usually occurs because deep inside we are afraid of the power of our feelings. We are afraid that we will be overwhelmed and that we will lose control. Super-emotionality also develops from the denial of our feelings. This is very curious but nevertheless true. We become over-sensitive if we are suffering from a backlog of unexpressed emotions which we were afraid to express at the right time.

Core Emotions

We have seen that when we are high in self-esteem we experience certain feelings and that low self-esteem is associated with other feelings. When our self-esteem is low we may feel:

uptight	depressed	critical
insecure	guilty	afraid of emotions
antisocial	worried	victimized

EXERCISE **Finding Your Core Emotions**

Look at the list above and choose three emotional states which you have experienced when you have been feeling low in self-esteem. Take one feeling at a time and write down any other feelings which are associated with it. Try to get right into the skin of the states you choose. Get right into the feeling, and the *feelings behind the feeling* will emerge.

For example, I may choose guilty. I write this down and then think about all the other feelings which I experienced when I felt guilty. I write these down.

EXAMPLE:

guilty ________ associated feelings: *anger with self* ________

________ *anger with others* ________

________ *resentment* ________

________ *fear of being found out* ________

1 ________ associated feelings: ________

____

____

____

2____________ associated feelings: ______________________________

____

____

____

3____________ associated feelings: ______________________________

____

____

____

Are there any associated feelings which recur? If so, what are they?

____

____

____

____

I call these recurring emotions our *core emotions*. These are deep feelings which lie *behind* our more acceptable feelings. The example demonstrates that perhaps it is easier for me to admit that I feel guilty about something than it is for me to recognize my feelings of anger, fear and resentment. If anger, fear or resentment appeared again during this exercise then I would know that the repeating feeling was one of my core emotions. Our core emotions are usually feelings which we find difficult to acknowledge. Do you find your core emotions hard to accept?

When we are high in self-esteem we respect our feelings and are able to express them appropriately. In this way we ensure that we are not being ruled by our emotions. When we can accept all our feelings we will no longer be trapped in behaviour which is extremely rational or extremely emotional. A healthy and balanced emotional life requires that we:

- experience a feeling
- recognize and accept this feeling
- express and let go of the feeling

If we don't go through this process we will experience a build-up of denied and unexpressed emotion. If we suppress our feelings for long enough we will become so out of touch with our emotional state that we won't even know what our feelings are any more; new feelings will be lost in our emotional confusion and so the build-up of unexpressed emotion continues.

Can you think of a time when a minor incident occurred and you completely overreacted? Maybe something quite sad happened and you felt overwhelmed by grief. Perhaps some small episode sent you into a great storm of anger. Whenever we deny our feelings, we cannot release them. We can never let go of anything until we have first acknowledged its existence. So denial leads to holding on, which means that these feelings we cannot accept are hidden away inside us. These secret feelings may be buried so deeply that we do not even recoguize their existence any more. Our secret feelings (hidden from others and maybe even hidden from ourselves) can create imbalance at all levels of our being: mind, body, spirit and emotions. Suppressed emotions lie within us just waiting to call our attention to them. They may erupt at some inappropriate time; they may cause us to become ill; their existence will always ensure that we are low in self-esteem.

How can I respect myself if I am denying my true feelings? My feelings are directly associated with my needs. If I am feeling good my needs are being met. If I don't feel good it is because my needs are not fulfilled. When I am denying my feelings I am denying my needs; I am virtually saying that my needs don't count – my self-esteem is at an all-time low!

Why Are We Afraid of Our Emotions?

As we grew out of babyhood we began to curtail the natural self-expression of our emotions because most of us learned, at an early age, that our feelings were best kept to ourselves. The root cause of this emotional denial lies in fear and we learned about this fear from the adult world around us.

- Feelings are powerful energy. *(How can we keep control if we are overwhelmed by emotion?)*
- Feelings are an expression of our needs. (If we show that we are 'needy' in any way we will be betraying our weakness and so will become vulnerable.)

Our culture abounds in familiar messages which encourage children to keep a stiff upper lip. Did you hear any of these when you were young? 'Boys don't cry . . . Don't be afraid . . . You shouldn't feel like that . . . When you get angry I can't take it . . . When you get unhappy I get unhappy . . . Don't cry – it's babyish . . . Just grin and bear it . . . Don't talk about death – it upsets people . . . Jealousy is so unattractive . . . Just pretend you don't care.' Can you add anything to this list?

These ideas may have been spoken messages or they may have been passed on in a more subtle way. We learn our beliefs about the way this world works in many different ways. Children often internalize messages which are not actually spoken out loud; the subtler messages of our childhood can nevertheless have profound effects in our adulthood. We have learned so much from the vibrations which surrounded our childhood. Thought, feeling and behaviour patterns permeate our lives and we experience them at every level; physical, mental, emotional and spiritual. We learn as much from what is left unsaid as from what is said. The raised eyebrow; the smile that never quite reached the eyes; a spoken acceptance with body language demonstrating rejection; the cold feeling which comes from being ignored. There are so many ways that we can learn from unspoken messages.

EXERCISE Unspoken Messages

What did you learn from the unspoken messages of your childhood? You may have to think very deeply before you can do this exercise; the messages may have been subtle but the implications will be profound. Look at the following example before you answer the questions.

EXAMPLE

1 The unspoken message was:
My father ignored me whenever I disagreed with him.

2 What I learned from this was:
If I always pretended to agree with my father he would give me attention.

3 The implications of this are:
I am now often unable to speak my mind and when this happens I feel very angry.

1 The unspoken message was:

____

____

____

____

2 What I learned from this was:

____

____

____

____

3 The implications of this are:

____

____

____

____

EXERCISE **Accepting and Expressing Emotions**

We all find some feelings harder to accept and to express than others. Fill in the Table of Emotions on page 34 to see what you find easy and what you find hard. Again, you may find the need to think very carefully before doing this exercise. Really think your answers through.

What did the Table of Emotions show you? Were you surprised by any of your answers? Look at the feelings that are always difficult to accept. Consider why you find these emotions so hard to deal with.

Maybe you learned as a child that these particular feelings were taboo in some way. For example, if you showed your love and then felt rejected, it might be too terrifing for you to show your loving feelings now. Perhaps you grew up in a very angry environment, where people were never able to release their anger at the appropriate time and so were always operating on the edge of a volcano of feelings. Some people are angry all their lives and they never discover the root of their anger. Such people may always be showing anger or they may show absolutely no emotion. Extremely hurt and angry people may eventually be numbed by the intensity of their own feelings. If we are really hurting we can try to defend ourselves by moving into a non-feeling mode. So, angry people may come in disguise and although they don't raise their voice the air may be thick with their numbed anger. Think about who was angry in your house and how they showed (or didn't show) that anger.

Did you find some feelings easy to accept but difficult to express? Although acceptance must come before the expression of a feeling, it doesn't follow that if you easily accept a feeling you will necessarily find it easy to express

TABLE OF EMOTIONS						
	Accepting			**Expressing**		
Feeling	Easy	Sometimes difficult	Always difficult	Easy	Sometimes difficult	Always difficult
Shame						
Sadness						
Happiness						
Anger						
Delight						
Grief						
Dislike						
Friendliness						
Fear						
Jealousy						
Worry						
Love						
Vulnerability						
Frustration						
Caring						
Aloneness						
Rejection						
Depression						

it. Acceptance is one part of the letting-go process and it is the first step. Sharing your feelings is something else. For example, perhaps I can accept my own grief but I might find it very difficult to express this feeling to anyone else. What will they think, or perhaps more importantly, can they handle it? 'Can they handle it?' is a big consideration.

Many people are very afraid of emotions for all the reasons which we have looked at. These folk 'can't handle it'. They send unspoken messages that say:

	1 Don't show me your emotions,
because . . .	2 I am afraid of your emotions,
because . . .	3 I am afraid of my own emotions,
and so . . .	4 I want you to deny your emotions and all will be well.

When you are ready to share an emotion find someone who *can* handle it. People who have done some work on releasing their own feelings find it easier to be a listening ear for others. You may feel at some stage that you need some counselling help or you might want to join a support group of some sort. However you can also work on yourself very effectively

EXERCISE Letting Go of Emotions

Use this process at any time when you are troubled by your feelings. It will help to clarify your true emotions.

Take an emotion which you find difficult to accept and to express. Write, 'I (name) am denying that I feel (emotion).'

For example, I might write:
I, Lynda, am denying that I feel ashamed.

1 I ____________ am denying that I feel ____________

Get a large sheet of paper, a pen, a mirror and a box of tissues.

Now write this statement over and over. When you have finished writing it then say it over and over. Notice all the feelings that are coming up for you. When you are ready, look into your own eyes in the mirror and repeat the statement. If this is hard *stick at it*: mirror work is a very profound experience. If you are feeling very emotional then express it in some way. You may have a bucketful of tears inside you; you may feel like beating the stuffing out of a pillow; you might just want to go to sleep. Do what feels right. You may be feeling unmoved and that's fine too, it doesn't mean that nothing is happening to you.

Continue the letting-go process no matter how you are feeling. Repeat the same process for all the parts of this exercise.

2 I ____________ am denying that I feel ____________ because______

____

____

____

____

If you can use the mirror then do so; this method is very effective. What is it like to look yourself in the eyes in this way?

3 I ______________ am ready to accept that I feel ______________

4 I ______________ accept that I feel ____________

5 I ______________ love and value all my experiences.

6 I ______________ love and value all my feelings.

7 I ______________ give myself permission to feel ____________

You are now allowing yourself to *experience fully* the denied feeling. If you are experiencing other feelings then acknowledge them. You may feel guilty or angry with yourself. If you do, then complete the following.

8 I ______________ forgive myself.

Do you feel angry with anyone else? If so, forgive them.

9 I ______________ forgive you____________

And so you can express your feelings in many different ways. Ultimately it is always a question of you yourself being able to to accept your feelings totally. When you can love and value yourself – whatever you may be feeling – you will no longer be at the mercy of your emotions. You will be respecting your feelings and will be able to express them appropriately. When your emotional life is balanced you are high in self-esteem.

Forgiveness

The state of forgiveness increases self-esteem.
The state of unforgiveness decreases self-esteem.

Forgiveness is a powerful way of increasing our self-esteem. When I first suggest to people that they might forgive someone with whom they are angry they usually say, 'Why should I when they did such and such to me? They don't deserve to be forgiven.'

Forgiveness does not mean that we say it's OK for anybody to do anything to us. Forgiveness is about letting go and we have seen the emotional effects of not being able to let go. If I cannot forgive you then my angry thoughts will connect me to you forever. You may live thousands of miles away, but if I only have to think of you for my emotions to stir me up then you may as well be living with me. And so it is that we can be bound in hatred all our lives to someone whom we may never see. We may even be carrying anger for someone who has died. This situation is not at all unusual.

Is there someone you find it difficult to forgive?

If so, the question to ask yourself is: 'What do I gain from not forgiving this person?'

You gain a permanent relationship with this person. You are bound together by your anger. Is that what you really want? Forgiving doesn't mean overlooking whatever happened or belittling your experience in any way: it actually means the opposite. Before you can let go of the ties that bind you to another person in hatred you need to look closely at what hurt you and why. You will need to express this in an appropriate way. When you can truly forgive, you set yourself free. How can you be high in self-esteem if you are hating someone?

The idea of forgiveness is closely bound up with all the work we are doing to increase our self-esteem. It will appear again and again in this book. You may need to remember to forgive as you do the next exercise.

EXERCISE Your Emotional Life

Answer these questions. They will help you to understand your relationship with your feelings.

1 Are you afraid of expressing any feelings? If so, what are they?

____

____

____

____

2 Why are you afraid of these feelings? What do you think will happen to you if you express them?

____

____

____

____

3 Is there anyone in your life to whom you could talk about these feelings?

____

____

____

____

4 Are there people close to you who you think would not want to hear about your feelings?

____

____

____

____

5 Why do you think that they wouldn't want you to share your feelings with them?

____

____

____

____

Look carefully at your answers to this exercise. What do they reveal to you? If you're feeling tearful or angry stay with your feelings if you can. Really allow yourself to feel whatever comes up and then the emotions will start to be released.

If you need to forgive someone, write your forgiveness twenty times on one side of a piece of paper.

I ______________ forgive you ______________

Write any feelings you may have during the exercise on the back of the paper. Affirmations bring up your negativity; this is the way they work. Don't be shocked by the things you have written on the back of the paper: remember you are releasing these thoughts and feelings. And if you haven't written anything on the back, that's OK too. Everyone reacts to these exercises differently. Do it some more, or try doing your forgiveness in the mirror (this technique is not recommended for the faint-hearted!). You may not want to forgive but if you are willing to try, the process will start.

You may by now be beginning to recognize a pattern running through your emotional life. This might be a repeating theme which is emerging. You may have no sense of a pattern but only of confusion. Whatever you may be feeling, remember that you are willing to change and this intention is a magic key.

- Say to yourself at this stage:

I ________________ am willing to change.

This is such a powerful affirmation.

Your present emotional experiences will link in some way with the emotional life you experienced in your childhood. We are always inclined to recreate the emotional relationships we had with our parents when we were very young. If we look at the ways in which our parents dealt with their feelings we may be able to see a pattern emerging.

EXERCISE **Your Parents and Their Emotions**

---

1 How did your father deal with his feelings?

____

____

____

____

2 How did your mother deal with her feelings?

____

____

____

____

3 How did your parents deal with their feelings in their relationship with each other?

____

____

____

____

4 What did you learn about emotional expression from your parents?

____

____

____

____

5 Are you finding it painful to think about your parents in this way? If so, can you describe how this feels?

____

____

____

____

Emotions do not *cause* pain. It is resistance to feeling which causes us pain. If we are afraid of a feeling and suppress it, we will feel pain. If we go with the feeling, then our experience may be very intense but it will not hurt us. Our feelings cannot hurt us; they are only part of our own self-expression. Your feelings have no power over you: you have created them. Enjoy them. They are an expression of your unique individuality, they are fascinating. *You* are fascinating.

Feeling Checks

Get to know your feelings. If I asked you: 'What are you feeling right now?' would you be able to say? Sometimes we confuse our thinking with our feeling and although they are closely linked they are not the same thing.

Give yourself *feeling checks* whenever you can remember throughout the day. Ask yourself, 'What am I feeling right now?' It will get easier and easier to answer. Learn to love your emotions and learn to love yourself.

4

How Do You Behave?

'We teach people the way we want them to treat us.'

How do you feel about this statement? Do you believe it or not?

More important than *what* you do is *how* you do it. If we want to achieve a satisfactory outcome from our social interactions then we need to learn to recognize certain behavioural styles. There is a direct link between our type of behaviour and our levels of self-esteem. If we are low in self-esteem then we act as victims. If we are high in self-esteem we make non-victim responses.

Figure 5 shows the range of behaviour which is open to us during any social interaction.

If we behave assertively then we are respecting our own needs as well as the needs of others and so of course we will have high self-esteem. Assertive behaviour requires that we know what we want; that we believe that we can 'make things happen'; that we are ready to take total responsibility for our own lives; that we take part in open and honest communication with others and that we are prepared to take a chance in life.

'Victim' behaviour can be *aggressive* or *submissive* or anywhere in between. If we are acting the victim then we are angry and resentful; we blame people for the things that happen to us; we have poor communication skills; we are afraid to show our true feelings; we are insecure and have no self-respect. When our self-esteem is low we can only operate in this victim mode.

The diagram shows a two-way arrow between aggressive and submissive behaviour. This is because we often swing between these two extremes. Something occurs and I feel threatened, I withdraw immediately into the submissive mode, hang my head and feel sorry for myself. I hold on to my resentment and then, at some point (and usually at a totally inappropriate time), I burst forth in an aggressive attack. Aggression creates alienation, it does nothing to facilitate clear communication between people. Consumed by guilt and remorse I swing back into the submissive style. Do you recognize this cycle?

Of course not everyone swings between these extremes. Some people specialize in the submissive style whilst others use aggressive tactics. At first

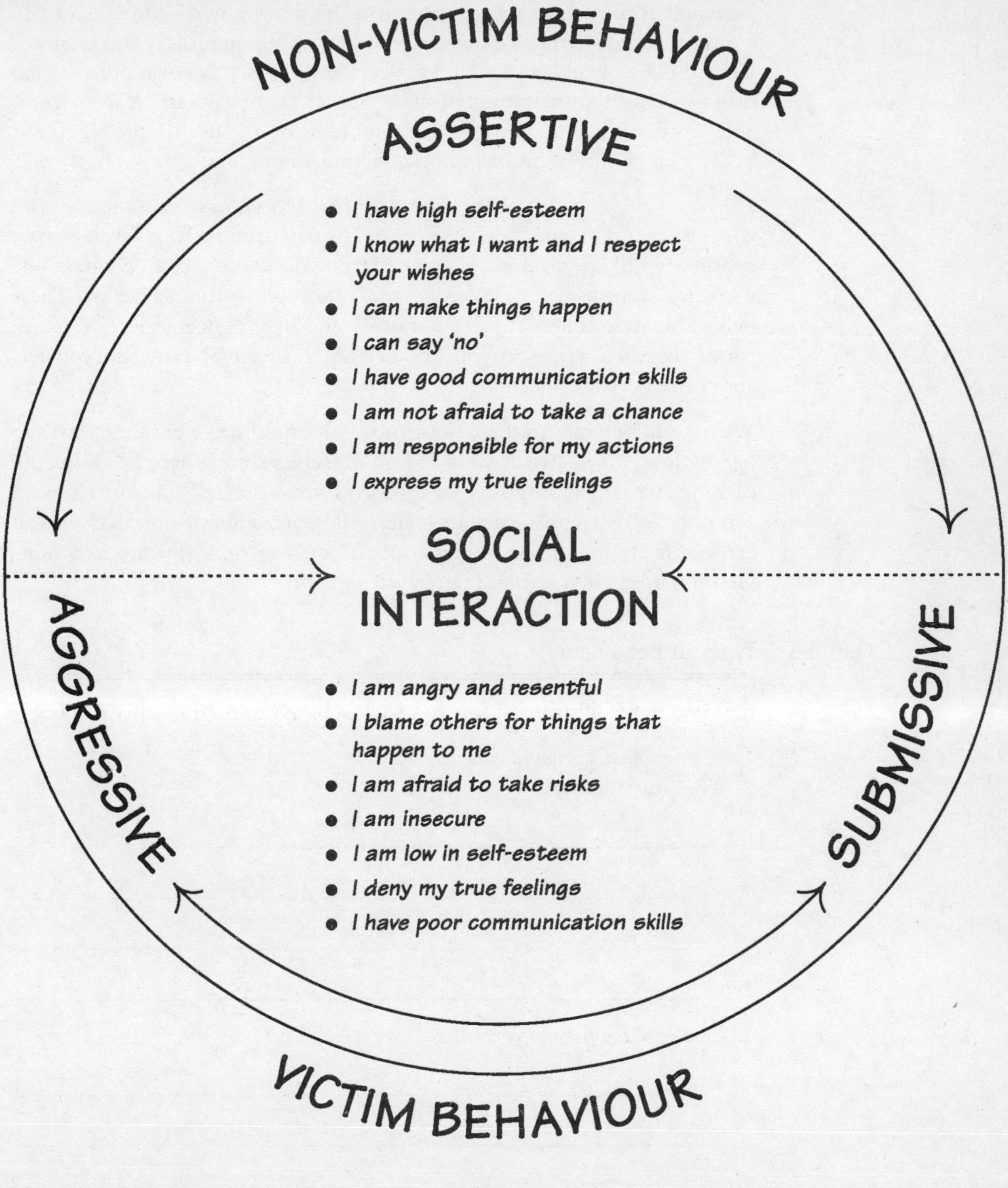

NON-VICTIM BEHAVIOUR

ASSERTIVE

- I have high self-esteem
- I know what I want and I respect your wishes
- I can make things happen
- I can say 'no'
- I have good communication skills
- I am not afraid to take a chance
- I am responsible for my actions
- I express my true feelings

SOCIAL INTERACTION

AGGRESSIVE

SUBMISSIVE

- I am angry and resentful
- I blame others for things that happen to me
- I am afraid to take risks
- I am insecure
- I am low in self-esteem
- I deny my true feelings
- I have poor communication skills

VICTIM BEHAVIOUR

Figure 5 Types of behaviour

it may seem that these two styles are completely different. An aggressor is loud and dominating and may appear to be determined and confident, in contrast to the submissive person who has a quiet approach and seems to lack confidence and direction. However, both styles are manipulative and blaming and they are both ineffective. Aggressive behaviour creates victims and closes down all purposeful communication and so the aggressor becomes a victim of his or her own victimizing tactics.

Do you recognize these behaviour patterns? Do you know someone who is aggressive? Do you know someone who is submissive? What is your relationship like with these people? Maybe you know a couple where one plays the submissive role whilst the other plays the aggressor. These behaviour styles often attract each other and they dance a merry (victim) dance together. Who do you know who is assertive? How do you feel about this person?

We have all behaved in these three modes at one time or another. If we are feeling low in self-worth we will find ourselves somewhere in the victim category, whether submissive or agressive; when our self-esteem is low we can only act as victims. When we are feeling good about ourselves we can act assertively and 'make things happen'; we can only operate in a non-victim mode when we are high in self-esteem.

EXERCISE Types of Behaviour

Can you think of a time when you have behaved in each of the three ways?

1 *A time when I behaved submissively*
The situation was:

____

____

____

____

The way I behaved was:

____

____

____

____

The outcome of the situation was:

____

____

____

____

2 *A time when I behaved aggressively*
The situation was:

____

____

____

____

The way I behaved was:

____

____

____

____

The outcome of the situation was:

____

____

____

____

3 *A time when I behaved assertively*
The situation was:

____

____

____

____

The way I behaved was:

____

____

____

____

The outcome of the situation was:

____

____

____

____

Are you a person who believes that you can 'make things happen' or do you think that 'things just happen' to you?

If you 'make things happen' you are assertive, confident and resourceful. You believe that you are the creative power in your life and you are high in self-esteem.

If 'things just happen' to you then you have given away your power to other people. You are a victim of the actions of others. You don't stand up for yourself and you are low in self-esteem. You may be a submissive or aggressive victim; either way you lose.

EXERCISE Victim Profile

Check your victim status by answering these questions.

1. A relative rings when you are very busy and you don't want to talk.
   A You take the phone call but you feel rushed and hassled.
   B You say that you can't speak at the moment but that you will ring back when you can.
2. You have been invited to a dinner party. You have eaten half the meal and you are full.
   A You carry on eating to please the hosts although you feel uncomfortable.

B You stop eating and explain that although the meal was delicious you can't eat any more.

3 Your doctor prescribes medication for what you thought was a minor complaint.

A You just take the pills.

B You ask what the pills are for, how they work, and if they are going to have any side effects. If you are unhappy with the answers you don't take the pills and/or you seek a second opinion.

4 Your family just drop their belongings around the house.

A You pick them up.

B You tell the members of your household that they are to put their own stuff away.

5 A double glazing salesperson rings at 7pm just as you are about to eat.

A You listen to her sales patter whilst your dinner goes cold.

B You tell her immediately that you are not interested.

6 You have just given up smoking and a friend is trying to persuade you to have a cigarette for old times' sake.

A You can't say no and take the cigarette.

B You say no and leave immediately if the situation is tempting you.

7 You are invited to a party. You don't like the host/hostess and you will be expected to buy a gift even if you don't attend.

A You resentfully buy a present.

B You politely apologize for not going and you don't buy a gift.

8 You believe that you have been overcharged by your solicitor.

A You just pay up to avoid a scene.

B You query the bill.

9 You have taken on too much and you can't fit in all that you have promised to do.

A You become irritated, resentful and angry and try to do a little bit of everything, ending up making a bad job of the lot.

B You delegate and find some time to relax.

10 You are coming home from a party and your partner is over the limit but insists on driving.

A You get into the passenger seat and worry.

B You insist that you drive or you call a taxi.

11 You have bought a new, expensive coat that your partner doesn't like.
A You don't wear it any more.
B You recognize that you have different tastes but wear the coat. After all, you chose it.

12 You are seriously trying to lose weight and you are out with a crowd who are trying to persuade you to eat fish and chips with them.
A You feel silly about the diet and 'go along' with the others.
B You say that you are sticking to your diet and go home if it all becomes too difficult.

13 You know that your teenage daughter is sleeping with her boyfriend.
A You hope that she is taking precautions.
B You ask her if she is using contraception and if she isn't you take her to a Family Planning Clinic.

14 The next door neighbours have the television on very late and very loud in a room that adjoins your bedroom.
A You wear earplugs and can't get to sleep.
B You go round and explain the situation and ask them to turn the television down or off.

15 Your boss asks you to work late and you have an important date arranged.
A You cancel your own arrangements and work.
B You tell your boss that you have a date that you don't want to break and that you don't mind working late sometimes but that you need some advance warning.

16 You have accomplished a good piece of work and someone compliments you.
A You say, 'Oh, it wasn't anything.'
B You thank them.

17 You decide, on the spur of the moment, to go out for the evening because you really need the break. A friend calls and asks if you will go round and babysit.
A You ditch your own plans because it is too difficult to say no.
B You tell her that you are sorry but that you have already made plans to go out.

18 You have booked a table at a restaurant, but when you arrive you find that you are seated next to the toilet.

A You swallow your disappointment and make the best of the situation.
B You speak up and ask to be moved. If there is nowhere else to sit then you leave and go elsewhere.

19 Your fourteen-year-old child is drinking and smoking. You are very worried about him.
A You don't like to say anything; you hope that he will grow out of it.
B You tackle the situation and tell him that he is too young to be making decisions about whether to smoke and drink. You demonstrate your concern and try to stop this behaviour.

20 Your mother is continually trying to tell you how to bring up your children.
A You are angry and upset by her intrusion but you don't say anything.
B You tell your mother that although you appreciate her opinion, these are your children and you will deal with them the way you think is right.

I know that not all the questions will be applicable to everyone, but maybe your answers will give you a feel for your potential to be victimized. How do you feel about your victim profile? Do you suffer excessively with the Doormat Syndrome?

The Doormat Syndrome

We all allow ourselves to be victimized sometimes; we all have our own particular areas of vulnerability. We may be able to assert ourselves at work but find it very difficult to do so at home with our families. Perhaps we are confident in the areas of our life which are familiar but find ourselves intimidated when faced with new situations.

Sometimes it is difficult to decide whether we are being victimized or whether we are just operating from the goodness of our heart. If a friend asks for your help and you have another engagement, what do you do? If you help her and cancel your own plans, are you a victim or are you a good friend? It can be very hard to decide whether your needs come before or after the needs of someone else; there is often a very fine line between being genuinely helpful and being a victim of another person's needs. *But there is a way to make a clear distinction.*

EXERCISE Victim or Not?

Think of a situation where you are uncertain as to whether you are playing the victim or not.

1 The situation is:

____

____

____

____

2 How I behave:

____

____

____

____

3 My feelings at the time are:

____

____

____

____

4 My thoughts at the time are:

____

____

____

____

Whenever you are in doubt about the nature of your actions look to the thoughts and feelings which you are experiencing.

Clues to victim status are to be found in *feelings* such as:

Fear
Intimidation
Anger
Resentment
Irritation
Helplessness
Low self-esteem

Clues to victim status are to be found in such underlying *thoughts* as:

I'm not as good as . . .
I want you to like me.
I can't say no.
I can't express my true feelings.
You are more deserving than me.

Look back at your answers to the exercise. Are any of your thoughts and feelings about your particular situation included in these lists or did you come up with something similar? The meaning of our actions always lies in our intention. What are my true motives? What do I really feel? Deep down you will always know the answers to these questions. It can be very hard to face the fact that we are doing something we don't really want to do. Sometimes we build our lives around the needs of others and once we start to recognize this we may unlock a volcano of anger which can feel very frightening. However, we don't have to do anything outrageous: we can change our situation by teaching our victimizers some new ways to behave around us.

Becoming Assertive

A non-victim response is an assertive response. We are assertive when we act in our own best interests and stand up for ourselves. We communicate our needs clearly and we also respect the rights and feelings of other people. We value ourselves and others and we are high in self-esteem.

We teach other people the way we want them to treat us by being open and honest about what we really want/don't want to do. How can you know my true feelings about a situation unless I tell you? Unfortunately, communication breakdown often occurs in long-standing relationships where one person thinks that they can predict the innermost thoughts and feelings of another. Sometimes we create a victimizing situation (which is of course characterized by its no-win nature) by *expecting* another person to know what we are thinking: 'I shouldn't have to *tell* you what I am thinking/feeling/wanting, you should just *know*.' *Never* expect anyone to know your needs and desires: you will always be let down, you will always be a victim. Just tell people clearly what you want. Communicate your needs. It makes life so much easier all round.

I have an acquaintance who is well known as a 'good sort' because she will do anything for anybody at any time. If I ask her to do anything for me she will say yes. She says yes to everyone and her house is always full of other people's children. She will *always* put others' needs before her own and she has no sense of her own worth. If we are denying our needs then we have a problem and we have very low self-esteem.

Another acquaintance, who is not known as a 'good sort' but is well respected has a different approach altogether. If I ask her a favour and she can't help me she will always say so.

Because she is able to say no, I feel much happier asking her. I feel I always know where I stand with her. When you know that you are 'using' a victim it leaves an uncomfortable feeling. Becoming a non-victim also requires that we become non-victimizers.

EXERCISE Changing Victim Behaviour

Think of a situation where you know you are being victimized.

1 The situation is:

____

____

____

____

Describe the ways that you behave in this situation.

2 I behave like a victim by:

____

____

____

____

What are your feelings whilst you are being a victim?

3 I am feeling:

____

____

____

____

What thoughts are you having when you are being victimized?

4 I am thinking that:

____

____

____

____

What messages are you conveying to your victimizer about your thoughts and feelings surrounding this situation?

5 I show the following thoughts and feelings:

____

____

____

____

Some Very Important Questions to Ask Yourself

Do your true thoughts and feelings match the messages that you are communicating to your victimizer?

This is a very important question. If your answer to this question is no, then ask yourself why.

Why are you not demonstrating your true needs in this situation?

Are you afraid of what will happen if you do express the truth?

What is the worst thing that can happen if you stand up for yourself?

Can you take responsibility for yourself or do you need to be able to blame someone else for what is/isn't happening in your life?

Is it difficult to say no?

Why is it difficult? Are you afraid that people won't like you if you assert yourself?

Do you care more about what people think than you do about the quality of your own life?

Now go back to your victimizing situation and change the script. By taking an assertive role how could you change your answers to question 2?

I behave assertively in this situation by:

____

____

____

____

How does this new answer affect the answers to the other questions in this exercise? Imagine the new scenario, see yourself in your new role and really try to get into the skin of the new assertive you, the you that is high in self-esteem. You can always use this exercise to help you when you are finding it difficult to assert yourself. Sometimes it may be very hard to face the real reason for the situation you find yourself in, but keep asking yourself those important questions and all will be revealed.

If you find, after answering question 5, that you *are* demonstrating your true thoughts and feelings about being victimized, then why are you still in this situation? If you know that you are being victimized and you are communicating your displeasure and your victimizer has not changed his/her behaviour then you have only two choices; to stay and be forever victimized or to leave.

Always remember that it is *you* who has allowed yourself to be victimized. There is absolutely no one else to blame. When potential victimizers enter your life you can teach them to change their behaviour and if they persist in their victimizing tactics then you can leave. Either way, you hold all the cards; you have taken constructive control of the situation, you have asserted yourself and have created a feeling of self-respect and high self-esteem.

Your present victim status will inevitably be linked in some way to the type of behaviour that you experienced around you in your very early years. What did you learn about victim and non-victim responses from your parents?

EXERCISE **Your Parents and Their Behaviour**

1 Think back to when you were a child. Did your mother operate largely in the victim or non-victim mode? What adjectives would you use to describe the ways that she behaved?

2 How would you describe the way your father behaved?

How do you feel when you cast your mind back in this way? Were you comfortable with your parents' behaviour or were you uncomfortable? Maybe you are feeling that discomfort now. Remember that your parents were always doing the best they could. We can only teach what we know, and if we don't know how to be assertive then we can't pass on that information.

And so a pattern of victimization passes from one generation to another. *You can break this pattern.* Forgive your parents; forgive yourself; forgive everybody; release all blame; take responsibility for your own life and pass on this information to your children. Non-victim consciousness means high self-esteem for everyone. When you change your behaviour you affect everyone with whom you interact. Victim behaviour creates victims with no self-esteem. Assertive behaviour creates mutual respect and high self-esteem. Go ahead and break the pattern. Create self-esteem.

PART 2

New Levels of Self-Esteem

5

Trusting Yourself

> The real voyage of discovery consists not in seeking new landscapes but in having new eyes.
>
> *Marcel Proust*

The ability to create new levels of self-esteem in our lives depends upon our degree of self-trust. If we can't trust ourselves we will never have self-belief, and self-belief is the foundation stone of self-esteem. If I believe in myself I will have self-respect, confidence and a positive outlook, all of which will help me to attract the very best into my life. If I can trust myself then others will feel able to trust me. If I feel respect for myself then I will gain the respect of others.

EXERCISE Reflecting Qualities

1 Think of someone whom you believe in, someone who encourages the confidence of others. What sort of qualities does this person have?

____

____

____

____

What type of relationship do you think that this person has with him/herself?

____

____

____

____

2 Now think of someone in whom you feel no trust and confidence, the last person you could depend upon. What sort of qualities does this person have?

What type of relationship do you think that this person has with him/herself?

We will always find that the people whom we trust and respect have a trusting and respectful relationship with themselves. Simply put, this means that such people value themselves. Look at a newborn baby: that birth is a miracle. Human beings are incredible and amazing. You are incredible and amazing! You were once that newborn baby. What has happened to take away your intrinsic worthiness? Nothing external has happened: the only change lies in your own perceptions. Self-esteem requires self-belief and belief in self requires that we trust ourselves. Look at the unconditional trust in a baby's eyes; what belief, what self-esteem!

Life is like a mirror: it reflects back to us our innermost thoughts, beliefs, perceptions and expectations.

3 What is your life reflecting to you at the moment?

If you believe that you are unlovable then your relationships will reflect this belief. If you feel that you don't deserve the best in life then, for sure, you will not get the best. Perhaps you feel that you are just 'not good enough' for . . .?

How can you trust yourself if you are feeling so unworthy?

The quality of your life depends entirely upon the quality of the relationship which you have with yourself.

Look at the checklist below

Trust Checklist

	yes	no
I believe in myself.	____	____
I usually know the right thing to do.	____	____
I trust my intuition.	____	____
I always do the best I can.	____	____
I learn from my mistakes.	____	____
I am safe.	____	____
The universe supports me.	____	____

Do you believe these things to be true for you? Most of our ways of thinking about ourselves and our world have been learned by us at a very early age. If your first few years of life were spent in a supportive environment and you were well nourished (physically, mentally, emotionally and spiritually) then it is likely that you will be able to contact a feeling of safety deep within you in your adulthood. If for any reason your early childhood was lacking in love and care and positive approval then you will probably find it difficult to say and believe that, 'I am safe' or that 'The universe supports me'.

EXERCISE Trust Checklist

Go back through the checklist and think carefully about the way you answered.

1 Why did you reply the way that you did?

2 What is difficult for you to believe and why?

3 What is easy for you to believe and why?

Positive self-belief requires that we *trust* ourselves and our world. Trust is a big word; it involves a commitment to holding positive beliefs about the universe at a very deep level; it requires an intimate relationship with our inner self. How can we develop an inner stability? Where can we start?

Trusting Your Intuition

Can you trust your intuition? Do you know what it is? Do you know where to look to find it?

One of the greatest gifts we can give our children is the awareness that they can 'look inside' themselves to solve their problems. How many of us were encouraged to look for answers within as opposed to without? Were you ever taught to listen to your 'gut' reaction or were you always told to 'reason things out'?

Our intuitive awareness is a bridge between the physical and spiritual world. We are more than our minds, bodies and emotions; we have a spiritual connection whereby we are joined to the rest of the universe. Our physical, mental, emotional and spiritual energies must be balanced in order for us to feel whole and well and in harmony. When our energies are balanced we feel centred and aware; we can realize our creative potential and recognize our intrinsic worthiness. We feel high in self-esteem.

Intuition is not logical, it is not reasonable and it is not predictable. You are tapping into your intuition when you have a 'hunch' about something; when you 'know' something to be true even if you haven't been told about it. Remember that time when you were just thinking about a friend and then you met them or they rang you? That's your intuition at work. What about the day when you threw out all your plans and did something completely different and spontaneous. Man (and woman) cannot live by reason alone; this world would be a dry old place if we were always ruled by our heads. However most of us have been taught to worship the God of Reason and so we need to work on ourselves to become reacquainted with the Goddess of Intuition.

If we live in a world of reason alone our energies will be out of balance. Our natural creativity will not flow and we will not feel good about ourselves, so our self-esteem will be low. On the other hand, if we live in the world of intuition alone nothing will ever get done; we will fantasize our lives away; our energy will be imbalanced and we will feel badly about ourselves, so we will be low in self-esteem.

The way to harmony, creativity and high self-esteem is through the delicate balancing of our intuition and our intellect. To achieve this balance most of us need to learn to recognize the voice of our intuition (we know only too well the voice of our intellect). The way to develop our intuition is to listen to it.

EXERCISE Listening to Your Intuition

Sit quietly in a comfortable position and take some deep breaths. Relax your body and your mind. Focus your thoughts on your intuition.

1 What feelings do you associate with your intuition?

____

____

____

____

2 Are these feelings welcoming or fearful (or anything else)?

____

____

____

____

3 Think of three times that you have followed your intuition and things turned out well.

____

____

____

____

4 Write down three things that your intuitive voice has been urging you to do. These might be only small things (for example, 'write that letter' or 'read that book') or they may be about bigger issues (for example, 'move house', 'end that relationship').

____

____

____

____

5 Why have you not acted on the advice of your intuition?

____

____

____

____

Intuition speaks to us through urges, feelings and flashes of insight. To hear our intuition we need to listen to our inner world of thoughts and feelings. Intuition always draws us to the things which give us energy and feed our creativity. What sort of future would you like for yourself? Would you like to do something entirely different? Perhaps you have a great desire to change your life in some way but keep creating excuses which stop you putting your plans into action. Maybe you are afraid to follow your intuition because it involves change and a certain amount of risk taking.

If you deny the voice of your intuition you will never be free to realize your creative potential; you will never feel balanced and centred; you will never feel high in self-esteem.

EXERCISE Relaxation

Take some time every day, even if only for a few minutes, to listen to your intuition. Find a quiet spot where you won't be interrupted, close your eyes and relax your body. Take some deep breaths and relax your mind. If you find yourself following your thoughts just observe these thoughts but don't get involved with them. Bring your mind back to focus on your breathing again.

In this relaxed and quiet state you can allow your intuition to come through. You may immediately recognize your intuitive voice or you may not. People tune in to their inner resources in different ways and we are all unique in our perceptions. You may experience strong feelings, you may not. Your intuition will guide you in different ways. There are no right and wrong ways of doing this exercise. Just keep practising and it will get easier and easier.

The most important part of the exercise is the strength of your intention to make contact with your intuition.

AFFIRMATION

'I trust my intuition.'

- Say this to yourself whenever you remember. It will strengthen your self-belief, your self-trust and your self-esteem.

If you have never made positive affirmations before you may find it difficult to make self-supporting statements. You may feel a bit silly, you may think it's wrong to say something you don't believe to be true. But this is the whole point of affirmations. We say affirmations to *change our negative beliefs about ourselves.*

If I don't trust my intuition it is because I have not learned to listen to its messages. We know how important it is to balance our reason and our intuition and so we practise exercises which will help us to hear our intuitive voice.

If I have learned to mistrust my intuition, I have made many (perhaps subconscious) negative affirmations: 'My intuition doesn't exist. How can I believe in something which I can't see? I was always told to stop day-dreaming. Fantasies get you nowhere. I can't trust myself to know the truth.' All these negative affirmations have created a situation which does not support me.

If I can't trust myself who can I trust? This world is a scary place without self-trust. If I don't believe in me I will always be low in self-esteem and my life will be a terrible struggle. Why should I continue in this way? There is a better way. I can change my beliefs. I can take a leap of faith and try a different way. What have I got to lose? And just look at what I have to gain.

- Suspend your disbelief, if only for a few minutes a day. Take time out to make the affirmation:

'I trust my intuition.'

- Practise the relaxation exercise and the affirmation for one week. If it makes you feel good, do it some more!

Change those negative beliefs that don't support your self-esteem for positive beliefs that do support your self-esteem.

You have everything to gain. Your life is just waiting for you to enjoy it.

6

Developing Your Spirituality

As we learn to develop our intuitive awareness we are becoming more aware of the spiritual part of our life. We are physical, mental, emotional and spiritual beings. These 'parts' of ourselves are not really separate – they are integrated and interdependent. To lead a fulfilling, satisfying and creative life we need to be able to relate to all 'parts' of ourselves. When the energy is freely flowing between our physical, mental, emotional and spiritual 'parts' we are having a balanced experience and we are high in self-esteem.

Every one of us is entirely different. What is easy for one person is difficult for another. We all have different skills and strengths and we all have different things which we find difficult. Some people find it very easy to relate to the physical world; they are very good at 'doing'. Some find it less easy to be action orientated – perhaps they are more in touch with their inner senses; these people may be good at 'being'.

We could say that our lives encompass the states of being and doing.

> *Doing* describes activity *out* in the world.
> *Being* describes awareness *within* the person.

As we have seen, high self-esteem requires us to balance all parts of our nature and this includes our 'being' and our 'doing'. Many of us are extreme 'do-ers' or extreme 'be-ers'. We are out of balance in some way and this is reflected in our low levels of self-esteem. Look at the following questionnaire to discover your levels of 'beingness' and 'doingness'.

QUESTIONNAIRE **Being and Doing**

	yes	no
1 I need to be on the go all the time.	____	____
2 I often have sleeping problems.	____	____
3 I am afraid to try new things.	____	____
4 I suffer from stress.	____	____
5 I am ultra-sensitive to others.	____	____

6 I find wordly matters threatening.	____	____
7 I am shy.	____	____
8 People think I am aggressive.	____	____
9 I have problems making relationships.	____	____
10 I am self-conscious.	____	____
11 I am a compulsive list maker.	____	____
12 I often find myself withdrawing.	____	____
13 I always like to stay in control.	____	____
14 I have a lot of nervous energy.	____	____
15 People think I am a passive person.	____	____
16 I'm not good at dealing with money matters.	____	____

If you have answered yes to any of these statements then you have a tendency to the extreme in either your doing or your being. Which way do you go when you are under pressure? Do you try to hide from the world by withdrawing (an extreme be-er) or do you hide yourself in excessive activity (an extreme do-er). We all fly to one extreme or another when we are under stress.

It's not wrong to behave in this way but it is of interest to recognize which way we are inclined to go. Any behavioural extreme will undermine our self-esteem. Balance is the key and if we can adjust our doing and being we create a balanced mixture of 'inner' and 'outer' activity.

Answer the following questions to discover where and how you can balance your being and doing.

QUESTIONNAIRE

High Self-Esteem, a Balance of Being and Doing

	yes	no
1 I like organizing.	____	____
2 I am at ease with people.	____	____
3 I know how to relax.	____	____
4 I am sensitive to others.	____	____
5 I am not afraid to try something new.	____	____

6 I like to nurture myself. ____ ____

7 I enjoy my work. ____ ____

8 I enjoy the subtle pleasures of life. ____ ____

9 I am good at making relationships. ____ ____

10 I enjoy inward-looking pursuits. ____ ____

11 I am comfortable dealing with financial matters. ____ ____

12 I can express my emotions. ____ ____

If you have answered yes to any of these statements then this indicates where you have balance in your life and where you are high in self-esteem. If you have answered no to all these questions, take heart – all is not lost. We can all balance our being and doing by developing our spiritual awareness.

Your Inner Awareness

When we look at our spiritual nature we are looking at our inner awareness. We need to ask such questions as:

- What is the quality of my relationship with myself?
- How can I get to know my inner self?
- How can I be responsive to my inner needs?

The first step of this inner journey depends upon whether or not you think that you deserve to devote time exclusively to your own needs.

EXERCISE Deserving

1 What do you deserve?

____

____

____

____

Do you think that you deserve to fulfil your dreams? Do you deserve the best that life has to offer? Do you believe that you don't deserve very much or in fact that you deserve nothing at all?

2 Why are you a deserving person?
or
Why are you not a deserving person?

Answer whichever question you think applies to you.

____

____

____

____

Examine closely your beliefs about what you think you deserve. Where have these beliefs come from? What did your parents used to say about what you deserved? Did you deserve a clip round the ear or a good telling off? What did your parents think they deserved? Did they feel that they deserved the good things in life? Perhaps they were disappointed by life; maybe they felt they didn't get what they deserved. Think about all the 'deserving' messages you may have received, whether spoken to you or picked up in more subtle ways.

AFFIRMATION

'I trust and respect myself and I deserve to satisfy my inner needs.'

- Repeat this affirmation over and over. Sing it, shout it, look in the mirror and say it. This affirmation supports your self-esteem and affirms a belief in your intrinsic 'deservability'. Say it enough times and it will start to take the place of any non-deserving messages you may have circling around your mind.

When we believe that we deserve to spend time on ourselves we are already on our inner journey. We can now recognize that we have inner needs and we can begin to respond to those needs.

Spiritual Nourishment

We can try to satisfy our material desires by 'doing' out there in the world. In fact most of us spend a large part of our lives in the quest to quench our thirst for what we recognize as the good things of this life. This thirst can never be slaked. The more we have the more we desire. The material world alone can never satisfy all our needs, because we also need nourishment of the spiritual kind.

Spirituality is hard to explain and impossible to define. I can only try to describe the feelings associated with a spiritual experience and hope that you can feel the meaning behind the words.

When we are connecting with the spiritual part of our being we experience a feeling of 'oneness' with the rest of the universe. This connection can be stimulated in various ways. Any event which totally concentrates the mind can bring about this feeling. Sometimes a life crisis can jolt us into a changed perception of the world. Our vision may be altered by the extreme nature of our experience and we are pushed beyond our 'normal' sensory perceptions. Has this ever happened to you?

Have you ever found that the hours have sped past whilst you have been 'lost' in some project which has taken your total concentration? Perhaps you have 'lost' yourself in a piece of music or in the beauty of nature. Whatever the cause, there is a common sense of 'losing' your old perceptions, seeing new connections and experiencing a 'oneness' which goes beyond mental activity. When the mind becomes concentrated and still, when the mental chattering ceases, then we can experience our spiritual nature.

As we have seen, this can 'just happen'. We can experience a shift in awareness because something occurs to draw us out of our normal sensory perceptions. However, we can consciously create this shift using any method which can still the mind. Some people know how to calm their mind with some relaxing activity; listening to or playing music; going for walks; dancing; painting or drawing; embroidery . . .

> Have you any relaxing activity which helps to calm and still your mind?
> Do you have any time to relax?
> Do you have any 'me' time?

Allocating 'Me' Time

'Me' time is spent on yourself alone; you may choose to be with other people but this time is not *for* others, it is just for you. The exercise that follows will help you think through what is involved in this personal time.

EXERCISE 'Me' Time

1 Do you have 'me' time daily? ______

2 If not, then why not?

______

______

______

3 Do you think that you deserve 'me' time? ______

4 If not, why not?

______

______

______

If you have answered questions 2 and 4, look carefully at your replies. What do they reveal to you?

If you find it difficult to allocate time for yourself then try, just for a week, to give yourself some time every day (even if it is just a few minutes to stand and stare). It might be useful to use the table on page 73 to record what happened.

What did your table reveal to you about your attitude to 'me' time?

Some people say that they feel guilty/selfish/don't know what to do with time for themselves/haven't got time . . . and so on.

If you haven't got time for yourself then who is going to have time for you?

5 If you feel guilty, whom do you feel guilty towards and why?

______

______

______

Look carefully at your relationship with this person/these people.

'ME TIME'				
When?	**Where?**	**How long for?**	**What did it feel like?**	**What did you do?**
Monday				
Tuesday				
Wednesday				
Thursday				
Friday				
Saturday				
Sunday				

Many more women than men find this exercise difficult. The important 'nurturing' role of the feminine often places women in a difficult position vis-à-vis relationships and in particular family relationships. I would like to say to all readers, both male and female, that:

> You are reminded that you must draw first from the well to nourish and give to yourself. Then there will be more than enough to nourish others.
>
> *Ralph Blum*, Book of Runes

Taking time for yourself is very important. If you want to develop your spiritual nature it is absolutely vital to allocate yourself some regular time to pursue this activity. As you find time to relax and to do things 'just for you' you will become increasingly aware of the spiritual side of your nature. As you develop spiritually you will balance your 'being' and 'doing' activities. This balance will increase your self-esteem and enhance your relationship with yourself and with others. If you find it hard to take 'me' time just keep trying. Extend the time each day and before you know it you will be wondering how you ever managed to live without it.

Creating a Spiritual Experience in Three Simple Stages

We can forge a direct link with the energy of the universe to experience a spiritual connection for ourselves. The intensity of this experience goes beyond relaxation of the mind/body/spirit. It takes us to a place deep within ourselves where we can meet our true spiritual nature. We can use a variety of techniques to make this connection. Disciplines such as t'ai chi and yoga, which still the mind, can open our spiritual eyes. Meditation techniques can put us in touch with the universal energy, but sometimes people find meditation a daunting prospect. If you find it difficult to connect with your spirituality, I can suggest a simple but incredibly effective approach.

Stage 1

How many 'you's are there inside you? How many different states have you experienced today? I have been irritated / pensive / happy / relieved / concerned / hungry / thirsty / emotional / joking / determined / satisfied / annoyed / thoughtful. . . and so it goes on, and on. We all play many 'parts' and who 'you' are will change continually throughout the day.

1 How many 'you's have you been today?

____

____

____

____

Once we are aware of these numerous 'you' states we gain a new perspective on ourselves. If we can stop identifying with our thoughts in this way we can 'give ourselves a break'.

2 Have you ever done something for which you can't forgive yourself? If so what was it?

____

____

____

____

The 'you' who performed this act is just one of your many faces. So, you made a mistake and you are paying for it over and over. Sometimes you can let one 'you' ruin the rest of your life. Get this in perspective; give yourself a break.

The techniques we use in stage 1 are *self-remembering* and *witnessing*. When we use self-remembering we become a witness of our daily life. The witness observes all that we do but casts no judgements. The witness creates an objective state where things are neither good nor bad, they just are.

EXAMPLE

You lose your temper with someone and then feel guilty about it. When you bring in your witness it merely makes a dispassionate note of what happened.

A *She is losing her temper.*
B *She is feeling guilty because she lost her temper.*

The witness is not emotionally involved in what you do, it just makes a note of what you do.

Put this book down, go about your business and witness your thoughts and actions. At first you may need to talk your way through it. For example: I am walking to the kitchen; I am feeling thirsty; I am making a cup of tea . . . Give yourself about fifteen minutes of witnessing time.

3 What was witnessing like? Was it easy or hard? Did you forget to do it? Did you enjoy it? Did it feel strange?

____

____

____

____

4 Go out into the world and practise witnessing. Try it anywhere and everywhere. No one knows what you are doing and the more you do it the easier it will become. I love to practise witnessing in a busy supermarket, it just changes the whole experience.

At first you may find that witnessing is easier when you are not feeling particularly emotionally involved in whatever is going on. Notice the occasions when you forget to witness: they will most likely be times when you were becoming emotionally 'hooked' into what was going on.

Use this technique whenever you remember. The more you use it, the more powerful it becomes. When we take the witness role we begin to create a calm centre within ourselves. This centre is a place where we can learn to break our identification with our transitory 'you' states; we can rise above our material and emotional attachments and so we can experience the true nature of our spirituality. As we learn to develop our spiritual nature we become balanced in our 'being' and 'doing' activities and so we increase our levels of self-esteem.

Once you have got used to the technique of witnessing it will become easier to experience being alone with yourself in silence. It is this process of being alone inside yourself which is really what meditation is all about.

Many people find meditative practices very hard to follow and this is sometimes because they expect themselves to sit for hours in pursuit of some mystical experience. To me, meditation is a very simple and practical method of getting in touch with my spirituality. The experience is never what I expect it to be and maybe this is the key – *to have no expectation of your meditation*. Spiritual revelations come in many guises.

Stage 2

Stage 2 requires that you sit comfortably in a relaxed state and close your eyes. In this way you remove all external distractions. Watch your mind at work; just let it wander. Bring in the witness to observe your thoughts and then to let go of them. Those thoughts will just keep on coming, so don't try to stop them. If you get hooked by a thought you will eventually recognize what you are doing and your witness can note what has happened and then let go.

There are no right and wrong ways to approach your spiritual development. Your intention to develop in this way is probably the most important factor. Self-criticism about the quality of your experience or the length of time you meditate will not help your spiritual quest in any way. Be easy on yourself. Remember that we are trying to love and value ourselves and we are not in the business of bringing ourselves down. Any time which you can spend alone in silence, observing your thoughts, feelings and emotions, is time well spent. Slowly but surely your spiritual nature will blossom and you will be amazed by your inner world.

Try stage 2 for ten minutes a day for a week and see how you go. When you are comfortable with this you might like to move on to stage 3 for ten minutes a day. If you wish to sit for longer periods then do so.

Stage 3

Stage 3 develops the inner process further. Sit as before and let your mind wander. Concentrate on the rhythm of your breathing. Follow your in-breath and then your out-breath. Be aware of your breath. As you breathe in think 'in' and as you breathe out think 'out'. In, out, in out. Each time your mind wanders off follow it, observe that it has wandered and then come back to your breathing. In, out, in, out.

Become aware of the place *between* the breaths – when you are not breathing in and you are not breathing out. Now concentrate on this place. Keep watching your breath but move your awareness to this place between the in- and out-breath. When your mind wanders off, follow it and then come back to your in- and out-breaths. Follow the in-breath and then the out-breath until you have regained a comfortable rhythm. Now return your concentration to the place between the breaths.

(The techniques described in stage 2 and stage 3 have been taken from my book *Creating Self-Esteem*.)

Practise these three stages. Become comfortable with one before you move on to the next. Encourage yourself at all times, especially if you are finding difficulties. Remember that the most important issue in your self-development is *always* the quality of your intention. If you really want to develop your spirituality then you will. Creating a spiritual experience in these three simple stages is an action plan which will work for you when you are ready for it and you will know when you are ready because you will enjoy the process.

As we consciously develop our spirituality we reinforce our feelings of self-respect. When our worldly 'outer' activity is balanced by our inner awareness, our 'being' and 'doing' are in harmony and we are high in self-esteem.

7
Increasing Self-Awareness

When the chips are down and things aren't going so well we often find our self-esteem is on the line (again!). When we are feeling vulnerable, rejected or criticized, how can we pull ourselves out of a spiral of negative self-beliefs which is fast 'proving' our 'worthlessness' and 'uselessness'?

We can always create self-esteem by involving ourselves in any activity which increases self-awareness. *When your self-esteem is low look to yourself for support. Look inside instead of outside.* This may be difficult at first; we are used to looking for someone to blame when things go wrong. *Blame always creates low self-esteem*; it will never enhance an experience because blame takes away your personal power. If you blame me for something which has happened to you then you have given me the power to affect your life. You have handed over the responsibility for yourself to me, you have become a victim and, by definition, you are low in self-esteem.

Do you ever give away your power by blaming others?

If you blame yourself and cannot find self-forgiveness in your heart then you have also disempowered yourself.

Do you ever find it hard to forgive yourself?

When you are consciously increasing your self-awareness you are getting to know yourself, you are really learning how to become your own best friend. How do you treat your best friend? You give her lots of support; you listen to her problems; you forgive her; you encourage her; you have a good time with her; you are there for her when she is up and when she is down. Think about yourself in this way, nurture yourself the way you would your own best friend and your relationship with yourself will blossom. Every time you learn something new about yourself you have increased your understanding of the way you tick. Self-knowledge is a door to self-esteem, as Figure 6 shows.

Figure 6
The value of self-awareness

Nurturing Yourself

Getting to know someone else requires that there is a certain level of trust between you. We develop this trust by nurturing the relationship. When we are trying to get to know ourselves we need this same level of commitment to the developing relationship. If I start to treat myself badly, being self-critical and blaming, the trust will be gone and the relationship will flounder. Self-awareness requires self-nurturing. What does it mean, to nurture yourself?

Think of the way you would treat a small helpless child. If the child was hungry you would feed it; if it cried you would comfort it; if it made a mistake you would forgive it; if it fell over you would pick it up and help it back to its feet. You would encourage this child in every way you knew. When this child falls over you don't yell at it. If the child drops a toy you don't criticize it. The child is free to make mistakes because that is how it learns. The child develops through love and support; it will not develop and learn if it is abused. Of course you treat this child well; it is only a child and it deserves your supportive love and care.

Do you treat yourself in this caring way?
Do you love and nurture yourself?
Do you help yourself up when you fall and comfort yourself when you are sad?
Do you forgive yourself when you make a mistake?

If you do all these things then you know how to nurture yourself. You are your own best friend. You are high in self-awareness and high in self-esteem.

I think, however, that you probably don't always treat yourself in this loving way. We often find it difficult to love ourselves; we find it much easier to be self-critical. Perhaps you get angry with yourself for not being 'good enough'. Good enough for what? Good enough for whom? Maybe you believe that you are not perfect and criticize yourself for all your imperfections. We are inclined to talk to ourselves in the ways people spoke to us when we were very young. Is it really any use to 'beat ourselves up' about our imperfections/mistakes/inabilities? When we are helping small children to learn, we encourage and support all their efforts. We all need encouragement; we won't learn and develop unless we feel supported.

Give yourself a chance: stop telling yourself off and try some self-nurturing activities instead. Recognize your originality and enjoy your uniqueness. Discover your own 'Inner Child' and learn to let yourself off the hook. As you get to know yourself and learn to enjoy yourself you will increase your self-esteem.

Recognizing Your Uniqueness

Uniqueness Checklist

		yes	no
1	When you describe yourself do you ever use the words 'normal' and/or 'average'?	____	____
2	Do you feel that it is important to fit in?	____	____
3	Are you attracted to originality?	____	____
4	Do you ever feel different from others in some way?	____	____
5	If the answer to question 4 is yes, do you ever try to hide this difference?	____	____
6	Are you frightened by change?	____	____
7	Do the achievements of others inspire you?	____	____
8	Do you ever feel threatened by other peoples' achievements?	____	____
9	Do you ever criticize yourself for not being 'as good as' someone else?	____	____
10	Do you aspire to 'normality'?	____	____
11	Is it important for you to keep up with present fashion?	____	____
12	If you are told, 'This rule applies to everyone and there are no exceptions,' do you give in?	____	____
13	'I am an exception': say this statement to yourself. Do you believe it?	____	____
14	Do you often wish that you looked like someone else?	____	____
15	Do you ever wish that you were someone else?	____	____

There is no such thing as the 'norm' or the 'average'. We have created these concepts in an attempt to categorize and structure our lives in some way. Structures and rules often play an important part in helping us to understand and cope with our daily lives. However, it is important to remember that standards and comparisons are not real measurements.

There is no 'normal' size or type of person. There is no 'right' way of doing things. If we are constantly comparing ourselves with a mythical 'norm', how can we evaluate our self-worth? Just buy this or that, or do this or the other, and you too will be as smart/look as beautiful/sound as clever . . . as whom? Do you ever compare yourself with others?

It is impossible to recognize your own intrinsic qualities if you are trying to be like everyone else. Sometimes it is very difficult to stand up and be different. Why do we struggle to lose our identity by attempting to be the same as others?

Our ideas and beliefs are culture bound, and indeed family bound, because as children we learn from others around us. If we ever feel limited in some way or vulnerable or at a loss and low in self-esteem we *always* need to look at our beliefs. What are we believing about ourselves and our world? Where do these ideas originate? Are we trying to be the same as, be as good as, be as talented as. . .whom? How can we judge our levels of ability, competence, awareness, cleverness? Only you can be inside you. Only you know what it feels like to be you. Only you know where you have come from and where you are going.

Everyone is facing different challenges and a course of action which will enhance your growth may merely be a limitation to someone else. Your strengths will not be the same as mine; my weaknesses will not be the same as yours. Our self-esteem is such a precious and fragile item and constant comparison will destroy it. To develop our self-esteem we need constant support and nurture; we need to recognize our intrinsic, unique worthiness. Love your originality, enjoy your differences, be yourself and you will create high self-esteem.

Tips on Celebrating Your Uniqueness

1 *Praise yourself for each success*, however small it may seem to be. Every step is important and it is so easy to dismiss the realization of our goals by moving the goalposts further and thereby creating a situation where we are never 'good enough'.

2 *Enjoy the unique qualities of others*. Recognize that every human achievement demonstrates the incredible potential available to us all. If we run a competitive race with others we will always lose. However hard we try, there will always be someone who can improve on our performance. Learn from the achievements of others and add what you have learned to your own experience. The human potential is incredible: enjoy the possibilities instead of being defeated by them.

3 *Enhance your originality*. Look at your differences and instead of trying to hide them make a feature of them. The places where you feel different are where you find the keys to your personal and unique creativity. The urge to conform destroys creativity. Whenever you feel the need to 'fit in' look carefully at what you feel are your differences. Accept and embellish your differences: they are what makes you a unique and original person.

4 *Accept your aloneness*. If we celebrate our uniqueness then we also celebrate our aloneness. Sometimes our aloneness may be very scary. We may feel lonely, that no one can ever really understand how we feel and always 'be there' for us. It's true, no one will ever know the inner you. You are the only person who can know yourself. No one else can be inside you. And would you really want anyone to know everything about you? The concept of our aloneness carries a quality of freedom. We can release our expectations of other people to know all about us and we can stop feeling guilty about not always being able to 'be there' for others. Limiting or freeing – your aloneness can be either of these things. Accept your aloneness and you will be free to be yourself.

5 *Do something different*. Have you been secretly longing to change your life in some way and been afraid to do so? Try it, whatever it is. Take the risk to be different and see how it feels. Self-esteem requires self-respect and it is hard to respect ourselves if we are running our lives according to the dictates of others. If there is something you long to do, give yourself permission to have a try. Life is here to be lived to the full – give your dreams a chance!

6 *Ask yourself, 'Do I really want to do this?'* whenever you find yourself in a situation which is uncomfortable. Maybe you are facing a challenge which you need to deal with in order to grow. But possibly you are trying to do something which you feel that you 'should' do and it doesn't feel right. Look inside yourself: only you can know the answer. If it doesn't feel right deep inside then closely examine your motives. Are you trying to please someone else at the expense of yourself? Is it worth it? Your self-esteem is at stake.

When we can enjoy our uniqueness we can recognize and respect the differences of others. Good relationships depend upon the understanding of our aloneness. When we can be happily alone we can be happily together with others. True togetherness depends upon acceptance of our aloneness. To celebrate your uniqueness is to celebrate your life.

Discovering Your Inner Child

My seven-year-old went to stay with his grandmother this summer and when he came home and we were emptying his case he picked up a T-shirt and said, 'This smells of Granny Mary's'. He was transported for a few moments back to the pleasures of his grandmother's house and, as he sat there in a reverie, I watched him enjoying memories which I knew he would never forget. The smell on his clothes was of pot pourri and polish, very indistinct to me but a powerful memory jerker for him.

We all have sensual experiences which can link us with our past. They may be smells, tastes, textures, noises, movements. Childhood memories can be rekindled by the touch of velvet; the taste of an aniseed ball; the smell of the sea; the sound of a church bell; a ride on a swing. . .

EXERCISE **Going Back to Your Childhood**

Are there any sensual experiences which take you back to your childhood? Can you fill in any of the categories below?

Touch ______________________________

Taste ______________________________

Smell ______________________________

Sound ______________________________

Movement ______________________________

If you have discovered any experiences which remind you of your childhood then *recreate that experience*. Go and eat a sherbet dip; look at the *Watch with Mother* video; ride a donkey; blow some bubbles; sit on a hay bale; play with marbles; go to a fair and smell the candy floss and even eat it . . . Your list may start very small but as you pursue these memories you will open the floodgates of your childhood experiences.

As you bite into that toffee apple you *are* the child within you. You may have grown up but your child does not go anywhere – your child remains with you. Your subconscious mind holds memories of all your childhood experiences from babyhood to adolescence – and these memories can be felt as powerfully now as they were in the long distant past.

Deep feelings of loss, unworthiness, guilt and shame can always be traced to our childhood, where, in the first few years of our life, we learned how to feel about ourselves. As tiny, vulnerable children we are open, trusting and totally aware, but as we learn to fit into the agendas of our parents and the rest of society we bury this vulnerability and total trust and build defences in order to 'protect' ourselves. Maybe we have been hurt so deeply that this open and trusting part of ourselves is totally buried. We could say that we have abandoned our Inner Child. If your self-esteem is very low then it is highly likely that you have closed the door on your Inner Child.

QUESTIONNAIRE **The Abandoned Inner Child**

Answer the following questions, scoring as follows:

0 almost never
1 sometimes
2 often
3 almost always

1 I am afraid to form close relationships. ________

2 I am irritated by people who don't 'act their age'. ________

3 I find it hard to trust others. ________

4 I can't express my feelings very easily. ________

5 I find it hard to have fun. ________

6 I expect the worst to happen. ________

7 I like to be 'realistic' about things. ________

8 Intimacy of any sort frightens me. ________

9 I am critical of myself. ________

10 I like to know all the facts before I make any decisions. ________

If you have scored 10 or less then you have done a lot of this work before. Most of us will score 20–30 in this exercise. Everyone has trust/intimacy/fear/shame/unworthiness problems from time to time, if not all the time!

Our Inner Child is vulnerable, and it is this very quality that enables us to form close, intimate and trusting relationships with ourselves, with other people and with the abundance of the universe. If we can reconnect with our abandoned Inner Child we can heal the deep hurts which caused our abandonment in the first place and we will be able to enjoy to the full the imaginative, creative and playful qualities of the Child within us.

All the exercises in this section 'Discovering Your Inner Child' may have an extremely profound effect upon you. Please take this section very slowly and dip in and out of it when you feel ready. The following section, on ways to reconnect with your Inner Child, is a particularly stretching list of tasks and it is advised that you concentrate on one task at a time until you have become fully used to all the different techniques.

EXERCISE Ways to Reconnect with Your Inner Child

1 List as many fun activities that you can think of which will help to reawaken your Inner Child. Think of things that a small child would enjoy doing, and then you do them.

____

____

____

____

____

____

Do at least one playful thing a day; the experience will grow on you.

2 Look out some photographs of yourself at various stages of your childhood. Put them in prominent positions around the house and look at them frequently. Get to know the way these children look; become familiar with their expressions. Make friends with these children and learn to love them as your very own: they are your very own. Each of these children is a part of you: reconnect with them and you will again assimilate all the amazing childlike qualities which you have lost in the process of 'growing up'.

If any part of your childhood is especially hard to recall then it probably means that this stage of your development was particularly painful. Try to find pictures of yourself during this time and discover all you can about this period of your life. Ask family and friends for any clues. Develop a close relationship with yourself at this difficult age. Repressed painful feelings may emerge and you might need to share these feelings with a trusted friend, support group or counsellor. Learn to love and respect all your Inner Children and you will be able to love and respect your whole self.

3 Take some crayons and a piece of paper and draw a picture of yourself as a child. Use the hand which you don't normally use. If you feel like it, go on and draw yourself as a child with your parents, and maybe the house where you lived. Carry on drawing if you are enjoying it, but make sure you use your non-dominant hand.

Picture of Me as a Child

4 Write a letter to your Inner Child with your non-dominant hand. Tell your Child whatever you need to say. Remember to tell her how much you appreciate her and love her; tell her that you want to be her friend and that now you have found her, you will always be there to support her.

Letter to My Inner Child

As your Inner Child becomes more and more trusting she will support your adult self with such imaginative and creative energy that you will become revitalized. Sometimes you may feel the hurts and losses which drove your Inner Child underground in the first place. Whenever you feel this pain, recognize that you are being healed and share the feelings if it is necessary; forgive your parents if you need to; forgive yourself if you need to.

5 *Visualization: Meeting Your Inner Child*

Relax in a comfortable position in a quiet place and read the following

'You are feeling comfortable and relaxed and you are in beautiful and peaceful surroundings. You are sitting with your back against a tree and you can feel the warm sun on your skin. You can hear the birds singing and you know that you are in a safe place. You look ahead and see a field of bright red flowers. They are poppies and they are swaying slightly in the warm breeze. You are feeling happy and contented and totally relaxed. In the very centre of the poppy field is a large leafy tree. As you begin to notice the tree you start to hear the tinkling of a bell. The bell sounds light and clear and very pure and as you are listening to this magical sound it begins to change into the laughter of a small child. The laughter seems to come from the tree and, as you look, you see that there is someone there. There is a child hiding behind the tree; this child is laughing but you know that it is very shy. You stand up and walk quietly towards the tree, so as not to frighten the child away. You see a little hand clasping the side of the tree; you touch the hand, very softly so that you do not frighten the child away. The child peeps out at you from behind the tree and laughs. You recognize the child: it is you, it is your Inner Child. You coax the child out from behind the tree and there she is, standing in front of you. You are so full of joy and happiness; your Child is so pleased to see you. Stay with your Child as long as you like. Maybe you will just sit with each other and slowly become reacquainted. You may have much to say to each other or maybe you will play together. Just enjoy whatever happens. When you feel ready to leave, embrace your Inner Child and tell her that you will be back to see her very soon. Your Child is smiling as you part, she waves goodbye to you as you walk away and she knows that you will come back to her.'

Return slowly Rub your hands together, stretch and feel yourself coming back into your body.

Read the instructions through again and then relax and close your eyes and create the visualization for yourself. There are no rules here: enjoy whatever happens. If your child won't come out from behind the tree then try again another time. Come to this place at any time you wish to meet with your Inner Child and get in touch with the playful, intimate and imaginative parts of yourself.

Please remember to approach this section very carefully because your relationship with your Inner Child is one of the most important relationships of your life. Cultivate it slowly and gently and you will enjoy a golden harvest.

Letting Yourself off the Hook

When I am working with a group I sometimes stop whatever we are doing and ask everyone to think of three things that they don't like about themselves. This exercise only takes a few minutes – everyone can think of *at least* three things and they are not reluctant to tell the rest of the group. Then I ask everybody to think of three things that they like about themselves. This is always so much more difficult, and most people can't think of one thing let alone three, and no one really wants to tell everyone else anything nice about themselves. Why is this? Why is it so much easier for us to bring ourselves down than it is to lift ourselves up? Try this exercise yourself.

EXERCISE **Things I Like and Don't Like About Myself**

1 Three things I don't like about myself:

____

____

____

2 Three things I like about myself:

____

____

____

Did you find it hard to praise yourself? Was it easy to criticize yourself?

Deep down we are all excessively self-critical; even the most seemingly confident folk have a well-developed 'Inner Critic'. The Inner Critic is that part of each of us which nags away at us and is *never* satisfied with our performance. You can easily recognize its voice; it is the one which tells you off all the time; the one that is never satisfied with your achievements; the one that keeps saying that you are never good enough/clever enough/-thin enough/educated enough to do or be anything of note in this world. The amazing thing about the Inner Critic is that it can *never* be satisfied and once we can understand this we can make great strides in increasing our levels of self-esteem.

Some Examples of the Inner Critic at Work

I decide that I will stay at home and look after my pre-school child because I think that she needs my care and attention.

Meanwhile, *at the same time* I am constantly bringing myself down for 'only being a housewife and a mum'.

I decide that I will go out to work and send my pre-school child to nursery because I want to work or we need the money or my child needs more stimulation.

Meanwhile, *at the same time* I am constantly punishing myself for not being a 'good enough mother'.

Do you recognize this syndrome? It is characterized by the following qualities:

Whichever way you decide to go you will lose.
Confusion and guilt feature heavily.
It will be very difficult to make decisions.
You will be low in self-esteem.

The work of the Inner Critic is never over: its job is to keep criticizing. Nothing satisfies it – it keeps you on the hook.

EXERCISE **The Inner Critic at Work**

Think of an example of the way that your Inner Critic is operating in your life at the moment. Look at where you are feeling confused/guilty/indecisive/low in self-esteem. The situation will be characterized by its 'whichever way you turn you will lose' nature. In other words, which hook are you hanging from? Describe the situation and try to be aware of the conflicting emotions which are involved.

On the one hand there is one possible way to act:

____

____

____

____

But there is another possible scenario:

____

____

____

____

These two possibilities are mutually exclusive. Whichever one you choose you will feel that you have made the wrong decision in some way. Shall I put my pre-school child into a nursery or shall I stay at home with her? Either way I am not satisfied. My Inner Critic ensures that I will be in a dilemma whichever way I decide to act. What can I do? What can you do?

Our Inner Critic is composed of all the criticisms we have had and believed to be true. If you are constantly bringing yourself down in some way, then look closely at what you are saying about yourself. If your beliefs about yourself do not support your self-esteem then change them. Criticism is not an effective learning tool. If I believe that I am stupid / lazy / worthless / not 'something' enough, how will I ever be high in self-esteem?

The key to change, development and high self-esteem is *acceptance*. We need to be able to accept all parts of ourselves. Accept that your Inner Critic will go on nagging at you (and occasionally it may have something useful to say). Learn to recognize the voice of your Inner Critic. As soon as you start to feel low, listen to what you are saying about yourself. Ask yourself if these things are really true or is this the voice of your Inner Critic.

You are an incredible, unique and amazing person and 99.9 per cent of the time you will be listening to your Inner Critic. Recognize this to be true, release your self-criticisms, forgive your mistakes and affirm your love and support for yourself.

AFFIRMATION

'I am doing the best I can. I am a valuable and lovable person and I deserve all the love and support that I can give myself.'

- Whenever you hear that Inner Critic knocking on the door of your mind say this affirmation to yourself. Remind yourself of your true worth and, if you do need to change in any way, this affirmation will give you the strength and support that you will need to make the change.

  Let yourself off all those hooks and you will be free to be the creative, decisive, confident person that you truly are.

As we increase our self-awareness we discover that we are so much more than we thought we were. The more we find out about ourselves the more we realize how incredibly fascinating we truly are.

Whenever you are looking for answers *look inside yourself*: you hold all the keys to the knowledge you need for your own self-development.

Love and value yourself, be your own best friend. This relationship will last forever!

8

Improving Personal Relationships

If only I could find the right man/woman I would be so happy. If only my parents would change then everything would be OK. If only my boss were more tolerant, work would be great. If only the children would behave better . . . Oh, if I could just change everyone I would be so happy. Whom or what would you like to change to make your relationships work? Fill in the following table.

THE WAYS I WOULD LIKE PEOPLE TO CHANGE	
Name	**I would like this person to be . . .**

We become trapped when we look for fulfilment anywhere *outside* ourselves. How can you change these people? The truth is that you can't change them and the more you try the worse it gets. Whenever we are waiting for someone to change we will be low in self-esteem. If your happiness depends upon the actions of others you have become a victim; you are disempowered; you have lost direction and self-respect.

Change Your Focus

> *The ways that people treat us are reflections of the ways that we treat ourselves.*

This is a wonderful liberating truth that can free you from the shackles of any relationship. Change your focus from the *outside* to the *inside.* Relationships are not made outside they are made inside. The only true relationship is the one which you have with yourself. All of your other relationships are a reflection of this one.

If I am high in self-respect then others will respond and treat me with the respect I deserve. If I love and appreciate myself then I will attract those qualities from others. Similarly, if I treat myself badly, others will certainly do the same. If I victimize myself I will be sure to attract the sort of people who are looking for a victim. If I am low in self-esteem it won't take much to convince everyone that I am not worth respecting and if I blame myself, soon everyone will be blaming me.

Relationships are made within us. This is sometimes very difficult to understand. We have been brought up on a diet of romantic fiction and similar mind-bending entertainments which have taught us to look outside ourselves for all the answers. Our search for Prince or Princess Charming will never succeed; we will always be disappointed. Just as I am writing this I can catch the strains of Marvin Gaye in the background singing, 'Too busy thinkin' 'bout my baby. Ain't got time for nothing else.' Not such a good omen for a relationship, but it is the romantic line we have been fed. Listen closely to the words of songs and notice where the focus lies.

When we change our focus there may be an initial sense of loss – a loss of potential excitement/danger/the unknown. Why are we so attracted to giving our power away? Perhaps it is because we really feel we want someone to take good care of us. The pattern of our present relationships is closely linked with the relationships we had with our parents. As tiny babies we are very sensitive to the emotional vibrations around us. As soon as we become aware of our parents' emotional pain, we try to make it right for them; we try to keep them happy so that they will be able to carry on looking after us. This feels like a survival issue to the tiny, vulnerable and needy baby and so, pleasing its parents becomes vitally important. Our future relationships will have this underlying theme. It goes like this:

> *'I will try to be what you want me to be if you will stay with me and give me what I need.'*

Do you recognize this theme in any of your relationships?

If you do then I'm sure that you know that this way of running relationships doesn't work. People can't always be what we want them to be and so we feel let down. We may then try to change them or we may give up, submit and become resentful, or we may leave and look for someone else who we think will give us what we need.

EXERCISE Changing Another Person

Think of a time when you tried to change another person.

1 The behaviour I wanted to change was:

____

____

____

____

2 I tried to change this behaviour by:

____

____

____

____

3 The outcome of this situation was:

____

____

____

____

Can you describe the type of relationship you now have with this person?

4 Our relationship now is:

____

____

____

____

Did your attempts to change this person have any effect on your relationship? If so, what happened?

5 Our relationship changed in the following ways:

It is only possible to make changes in a relationship if you yourself are prepared to change the messages that you are sending to the other person. If you are focusing on the other person, you are looking in the wrong direction!

EXERCISE Choosing to Stay in a Poor Relationship

Have you ever stayed in an unhappy relationship? If so, can you describe it?

1 This relationship is/was unsatisfactory because:

2 I tried to change this relationship. yes/no

3 I chose to stay in this relationship because:

4 My feelings about the other person in the relationship are:

____

____

5 I am still in this relationship. yes/no

6 My feelings about myself are:

____

____

____

____

7 I would describe myself as being high/low in self-esteem.

If you have tried unsuccessfully to change the nature of a relationship and you still find yourself involved then look closely at your motives. Are you living out the underlying theme which you developed with your parents when you were a baby. Do you need to please people, do you need to be 'looked after'?

There is a double irony in this situation. Firstly, we can hardly feel 'looked after' within an unhappy relationship and secondly, what we are most looking for *outside* ourselves is the caring and nurturing which only we personally can provide. We are no longer babies, we can take responsibility for our own care.

Checking Your Relationships – Are They Healthy?

A healthy relationship is one that allows us to satisfy our own basic needs, and a useful way to recognize these needs is to become aware of our personal boundaries. A boundary or limit is the distance we can comfortably go in a relationship. These boundaries exist at all levels of our being: spiritual, mental, physical, emotional.

Once we become aware of our boundaries we have an insight into who we are and what we want. Looking at our boundaries is another way of becoming self-aware and, as we know, the more we are aware of ourselves, the more positive and resourceful we can be in our lives. Until I know who I am and what I want it will be impossible to know what is right for me and what is not right. I will be unable to have a healthy relationship of any sort with you (casual, close or intimate) because I won't know where I end and you begin.

And stand together yet not too near together:
For the pillars of the temple stand apart,
And the oak tree and the cypress grow not in
each other's shadow.

Kahlil Gibran, The Prophet

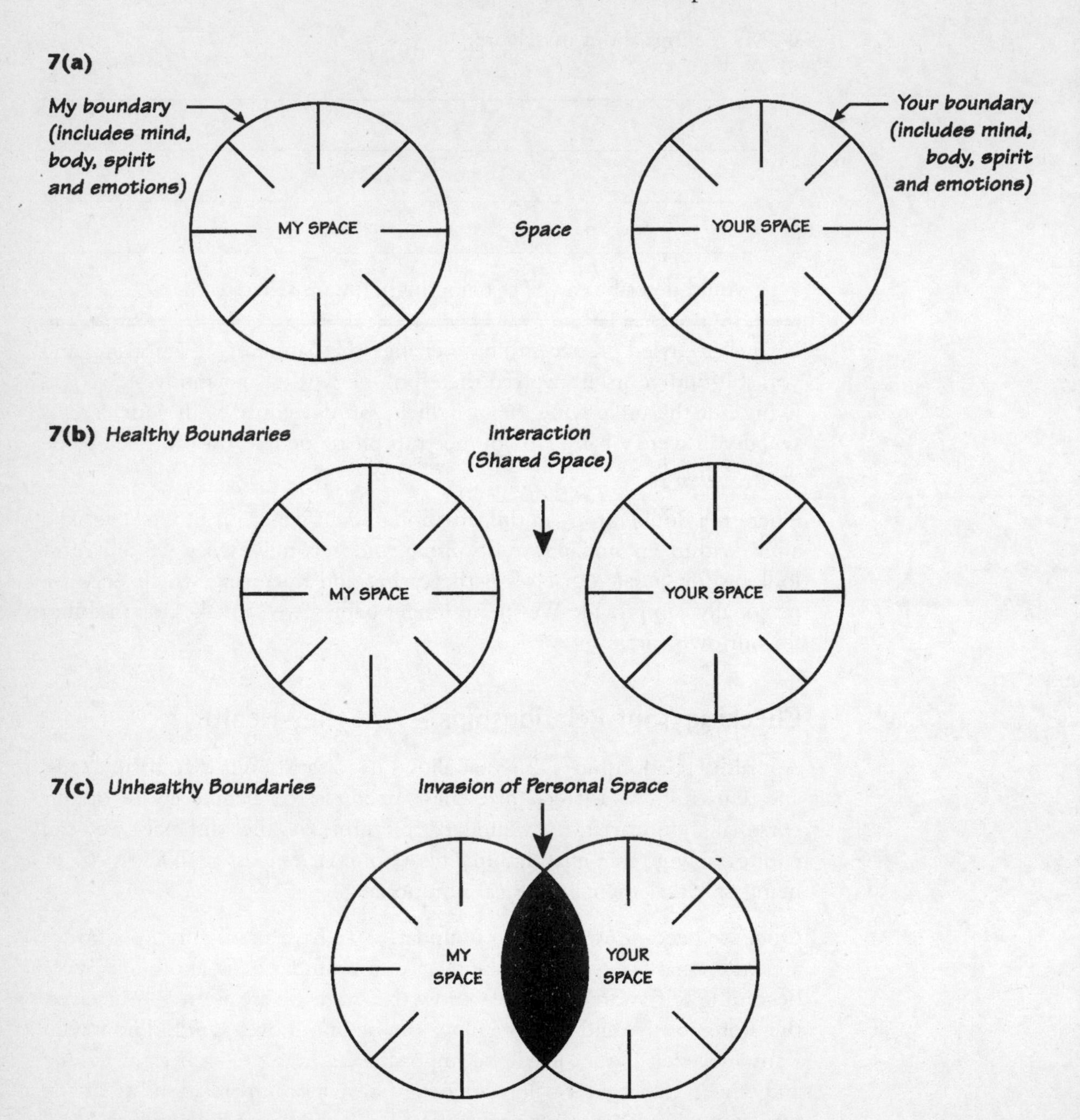

Figure 7 Healthy and unhealthy boundaries

Figure 7 is a diagrammatic representation of a meeting between you and me. Diagram (a) shows you and me just as we are appearing in each other's lives. Our separate boundaries represent the totality of our being – mind, body, spirit and emotions. Space lies between us. Diagram (b) shows us coming together and interacting. We are sharing some space but our boundaries are intact and we are having a healthy relationship. Diagram (c) shows an invasion of boundaries: our personal limits have been blurred. My boundaries and yours have become intermixed; the relationship is unhealthy because neither of us has a true sense of self any more. Where do I end and you begin? Do I want this or are we doing it because you want to? Look at the boundary checklist to see how healthy your own boundaries are.

Boundary Checklist

Answer the following questions, using these options:

- Untrue
- Sometimes true
- Often true
- True

1 I put others' needs before my own. ________

2 I am good at making decisions. ________

3 I feel responsible for other people. ________

4 People seem to take me for granted. ________

5 I find it difficult to express my true feelings. ________

6 I seem to put a lot into my relationships and get very little back. ________

7 I am able to speak my mind. ________

8 I feel used by other people. ________

9 I like to make people feel good. ________

10 I am not victimized by other people. ________

11 I am frightened by angry feelings. ________

12 I make relationships with people who are no good for me. ________

13 I feel upset if other people are upset. ____________

14 I am afraid to spend time alone. ____________

15 Criticism really hurts me. ____________

16 I will not stay in abusive relationships. ____________

17 I don't trust myself. ____________

18 I am very sensitive to the moods of others. ____________

19 I find it difficult to keep a secret. ____________

20 I can enjoy the successes of others. ____________

Think about how each of your answers affects the quality of your relationships. Look in particular at the behaviour and feelings which you think create a problem in your interactions with others: these are the areas where your boundaries are weak. Wherever you have a boundary problem you will also have low self-esteem. Poor relationships, unhealthy boundaries and low self-esteem go hand in hand.

Victims are blamers who, for some reason or other (usually fear), will not take responsibility for themselves. If you are in an unsatisfactory relationship and you are blaming the other person, you are a victim. Change your focus, look at your own behaviour, check your boundaries, take responsibility for your own needs and the quality of your relationships will change dramatically. Increase your self-awareness and your self-esteem will increase in equal measure. Increase your self-esteem and you will attract healthy relationships. Attract healthy relationships and your self-respect, confidence and self-esteem will take a further boost. Relationships are made *inside* and not *outside* and, as soon as you change your focus, you begin a process which can only increase your self-esteem and enhance the quality of your relationships. Figure 8 shows how this works.

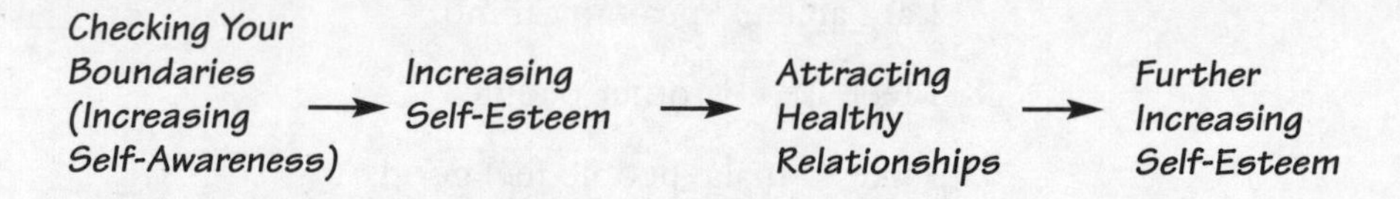

Figure 8 Changing your focus

AFFIRMATION You are a wonderful, caring and loving person who deserves to have supportive and nurturing relationships.

- Write this affirmation over and over again. Look into a mirror and say it to yourself.

'I . . . (your name) . . . am a wonderful, caring and loving person and I deserve to have supportive and nurturing relationships.'

The relationship you have with yourself is *the* relationship of your life. All others are only a reflection of this relationship, so make it a good one!

9

Increasing Prosperity and Wealth

> Prosperous (adj.): 1 flourishing; prospering. 2 rich; affluent; wealthy 3 favourable or promising.
>
> Collins English Dictionary

I love the word 'prosperous'. It sounds so full of well-being and self esteem. Do you feel prosperous?

A person may be rich in money but insecure about how to hang on to it, afraid of being robbed, or engulfed by guilt and totally unable to enjoy his wealth. On the other hand someone else who has less money may know how to enjoy what he has and to make the very best of his life. Who is flourishing? Who is prosperous? Which life is favourable? Who is high in self-esteem? Prosperity consciousness does not depend on your wealth but rather your wealth depends on your prosperity consciousness. Feel rich in the good things of life and they will be attracted to you. Feel poor in your resources and so you will remain. Is your universe overflowing and abundant or is it impoverished and characterized by scarcity?

QUESTIONNAIRE

My World View

Put 'I believe that. . .' before each question and answer yes or no.

	yes	no
1 This is a world of plenty.	____	____
2 There will never be enough of everything to satisfy everybody.	____	____
3 The world is a safe place.	____	____
4 People are starving, the world is running out of food.	____	____
5 The universe supports me.	____	____
6 Human nature is basically competitive and not cooperative.	____	____
7 We have the power to transform the planet.	____	____

8 We deserve an ecological disaster because of the way we abuse the Earth.	____	____
9 Everyone looks after number one.	____	____
10 I create my own reality.	____	____
11 My life is a struggle, we are here to suffer.	____	____
12 We all deserve the very best in life.	____	____
13 Nothing I can do will change the world.	____	____

Is your world a scary place? Do you live in an abundant universe or are you steeped in scarcity consciousness? Which way of looking at the world supports your self-esteem and makes you feel good? Which view of the world allows for the possibility of change and which one ensures that you will remain a victim?

It is true that people are starving and dying in wars. Yes, the planet abounds in toxic waste; the seas are being poisoned; the rainforests are being cut down; and there are holes in the ozone layer. This is certainly the way things are, but why are they like this? There is a growing opinion that a mass belief in scarcity has created our planetary problems. Humanity holds a mass belief that 'there will never be enough of anything to go round', and so we must fight for scarce resources and compete for our survival. We have created scarcity: it is only an idea. This universe is abundant. It has everything that we need.

We have created scarcity – let us create prosperity instead.

If we can change our individual consciousness to one of prosperity instead of scarcity, we will attract new energy into our lives. Think prosperous and you will start to feel prosperous; feel prosperous and you will affect the energy of those around you.

The following list shows the type of beliefs which create prosperity consciousness and the type of beliefs which create scarcity consciousness. These statements are *affirmations of beliefs*. Beware of the words you use: they create your beliefs. Change the beliefs that aren't working for you. Increase your prosperity consciousness by repeating the affirmations in column A. Whenever you are feeling impoverished in any way, choose some of these prosperity affirmations and say them or sing them or write them. Expand your vision, embrace the benevolent energy of the universe and allow abundance to flow into your life.

Affirmations of Prosperity, Affirmations of Scarcity

A	B
Prosperity consciousness	**Scarcity consciousness**
I believe that. . .	*I believe that. . .*
The more I give, the more I will receive.	Life is disappointing.
Life is a celebration.	Human nature is basically competitive.
I can change my reality.	I am a victim of circumstances.
I deserve the best in life.	We are a naturally violent species.
We are here to take care of each other.	Global destruction has gone too far to be redeemed.
My beliefs create the quality of my life.	Events are outside my control.
We can heal the planet.	Spiritual awareness offers no practical answers.
Self-transformation leads to global transformation.	I am insignificant in the grand scheme of things.
There is always enough of everything to go round.	Our resources are running out.
We are all connected.	We deserve a global disaster.
Nature has abundant resources.	The more I give, the less I have.
Scarcity is an idea that we have created.	There is no meaning to life other than to survive.
We are here to learn and grow.	'Positive thinking' is unrealistic.
Fear is the greatest destructive force.	The world is full of evil.
Love and respect are infinite resources.	My beliefs are true; they cannot be changed.
My high self-esteem enhances the lives of others.	My low self-esteem is not of interest to anyone else.
Mutual self-esteem can create global prosperity.	Scarcity exists, it is the only reality.

Read column A and then read column B. Notice any changes in your energy and mood as you read these statements. Which beliefs were energizing and uplifting? Which were depressing and lowering? Always follow the course which increases your feelings of 'aliveness' and prosperity. Trust your intuition. Endorse hope instead of hopelessness. Whilst we believe that we are victims of a system that we cannot change, we give away our creative power. Harness your amazing creative gifts; affirm prosperity consciousness; feel prosperous and increase your self-esteem; change the quality of your life and so help change the quality of the lives of others. Global prosperity consciousness will heal our planet.

Recognizing the Abundance of the Universe

AFFIRMATION

'The abundance of the universe is mine.'

- Say this affirmation to yourself. Never mind if you don't believe it at first. Just let those negative thoughts go. They won't work for you. They won't increase your prosperity or your self-esteem.

Experience the abundance of the universe. There is so much of everything. Open a tomato and see how many seeds are inside, so many babies from one fruit. Blow a dandelion clock and watch the seeds fly: how many potential dandelions can you see? The world is naturally prolific. There is no shortage of air, unless we decide to pollute it. Everything in nature is in harmony and balance unless we decide to create imbalance. Go out and look for abundance and prosperity and you will see it everywhere. The more you become open to this abundance, the more you will attract, and this awareness will reach out to those around you. The people who are ready to change their consciousness will pick up on your new thought patterns. Prosperity consciousness begets prosperity consciousness. Whatever you believe to be true will come true for you in some way. So change your scarcity beliefs, make plenty of affirmations for prosperity.

Awareness of abundance and prosperity consciousness can change the planet. We don't need to compete: we can co-operate. There is plenty of everything to go round. If our world governments abounded in abundance awareness just think how we could all prosper and flourish – we could change the world, and we will!

Prosperity and Money

Prosperity issues are always about the quality of our individual lives and so increasing prosperity may mean different things to each one of us. We can be wealthy and not feel prosperous because prosperity is a feeling of aliveness, of well-being, of self-respect and self-esteem, and money cannot buy these things. What does prosperity mean to you? Are you rich in success, in relationships, in health, in awareness? Perhaps having more money would mean an increase in your prosperity.

What is money? Money has no intrinsic value. It is only a symbol which we use to exchange the products of our creative energy. But it is related to other concerns, such as:

- how much we earn
- how we earn it
- how we spend it
- resentment for not having enough
- guilt for having too much

Money and its related issues – making it, having too much of it, having too little of it – are all incredibly controversial subjects. Any discussion of money issues very quickly becomes emotionally charged. Money is an emotional subject because at one level it can be seen as a measure of our material worth. If we don't earn enough money to feel prosperous then this will affect our self-esteem. How can I feel self-worth if my creative energy is not valued? In other words, if my labour cannot provide me with a comfortable living then my sense of value and worth may be affected. When I work with the unemployed I meet self-esteem at an all-time low. However, high self-esteem and wealth are not always linked. I know rich people who are very insecure and unhappy. The vital connection between our self-esteem and money lies in our beliefs about money. Check your own beliefs in the following questionnaire.

QUESTIONNAIRE

My Beliefs About Money

Which of these statements do you believe?

1 Money is dirty.

2 Truly creative people will never get rich.

3 You can make a lot of money only if you cheat people.

4 I am poor but honest.

5 If I had money I would feel guilty about it.

6 You get money only if you work really hard.

7 If I were successful at making money, some people might not like me any more.

8 Money doesn't grow on trees.

9 People with money are mean.

10 I wouldn't know what to do with a lot of money.

11 My parents were poor and I am the same.

12 If I got rich it might take me away from my spiritual path.

13 If I had money I would never be able to know who were my true friends.

None of these beliefs will help you to attract money into your life. In fact they will do just the reverse.

Which statements do you believe? Where did your beliefs about money come from?

EXERCISE **Your Feelings, Thoughts and Actions in Relation to Money**

1 My biggest worry related to money is:

____

____

____

____

2 What did your parents believe about money?

____

____

____

____

3 How were money matters handled in your family?

____

____

____

____

4 How do you deal with money matters now?

____

____

____

____

5 Would you like to change the ways that you handle financial matters? If so, what would you like to change?

____

____

____

____

6 Have you any beliefs about money that you would like to change?

____

____

____

____

What has this exercise revealed to you? Are there any links between your beliefs, actions and feelings and those of your parents? What would you like to change in your relationship with money?

ACTION PLAN: Changing My Money Consciousness

A Take any limiting feelings/actions/thoughts related to money.

B Look for the belief behind these limitations.

C Making positive affirmations which support feelings of expansion and prosperity.

D Ask yourself why you might be hanging on to these limitations.

E Affirm that you are ready to change.

Use action plan steps A, B, C, D and E to change limiting beliefs.

EXAMPLE:

A Action: *I am very mean; I only buy things which are reduced.*

B Belief: *I am a poor person.*

C Affirmation: *I am rich in the abundance of the universe.*

D *I have been hanging on to this belief because if I am a poor person people won't feel threatened by me and so they will like me.*

E Affirmation: *I am now ready to change.*

EXERCISE My Action Plan

A Take any limiting thought/action/feeling that you have discovered which affects your money consciousness. Write it here.

____

____

____

____

B What is the belief which lies at the root of this limitation?

____

____

____

____

C Make an affirmation which contradicts this belief.

____

____

____

____

D I have been hanging on to this limitation because:

____

____

____

____

E Write the affirmation, 'I am now ready to change'.

____

Use this action plan to help you unearth and change the sources of any of your limiting money-consciousness patterns.

If this exercise brought to light any childhood messages which you believe are affecting you now, then *forgive* your parents. They are not to blame: they were limited by what they had learned from *their* parents.

Let go of the past and move forward into a prosperous and abundant universe. When you truly believe that you deserve to have all the money you need it will come to you.

Increasing Your Wealth

We have seen how high self-esteem is linked with being balanced. When our 'doing' and 'being' are balanced then our mind, body, spirit and emotions are in harmony and we are using our whole self to create our lives. In terms of increasing our wealth this might entail taking active steps to look for a job or to create work for ourselves by going out, taking risks, making decisions – whatever we need to do. However there are other ways to act which belong to the 'being' part of our nature and these *inner ways* can produce amazing results in the area of making money.

Manifesting

Form follows thought. This means that whatever we create in our lives was once just a thought. Your house was once a thought in an architect's mind; your dinner was a thought before you made it; this book was a thought before I wrote it. This is such an obvious idea and yet it has profound consequences.

Imagine your thoughts as magnets. As you send out your thoughts you are sending out magnets into the world. These magnets attract their duplicates in material form – *thoughts are things*, so watch what you are thinking. If, deep down, you can't believe that you deserve something then you can be sure that you will never get it – you are sending out 'not deserving' magnets and that is the reality which will manifest. So you need to get very clear about your money beliefs so that your thought magnets are carrying messages which will attract money into your life rather than repel it.

EXERCISE

Manifesting My Heart's Desire

Expand your thoughts by developing your imagination. Think of what you would most like to happen in your life. If thoughts come up (like 'that's impossible') just ignore them for once. (What have such thoughts ever done for you?) Concentrate on possibilities. Think big, push back your boundaries, change your expectations, be creative. Enjoy this exercise.

Write down all the things that you would like to manifest. Remember that your thoughts are magnets so be as clear as you can about your thinking.

Keep playing with these ideas as you go about your daily business. Have a strong, clear intention to get what you want and make the possibility of it as real as you can. Focus on your outcome and this will eventually attract the ways and means into your life.

Close your eyes and visualize your outcome; really feel and taste your success. See yourself achieving your goal. Make your visualization as real as possible.

The power of your thoughts, expectations and visualizations is creating your life at every moment. What are you creating? Are you flourishing and prospering? Are you high in self-esteem? What are your thought magnets attracting into your life? What are they repelling from your life? Watch your thoughts; make powerful positive affirmations; visualize these affirmations in action and consciously manifest your heart's desire.

10
Healing Your Life

'To heal' literally means 'to make whole'. Because we exist at the mental, spiritual, physical and emotional levels, our personal healing always involves balancing these aspects of ourselves. Figure 9 demonstrates how these four interrelated aspects come together to create our whole self. When we *are* balanced, our energy is flowing freely, our mental, physical, emotional and spiritual energies are in harmony and we are 'at ease'. If, for some reason, there is a block in the circuit, and this can be in any one or more of the levels, then we become out of balance, we are dis-eased (not at ease) and eventually we become diseased in some way

Figure 9
The whole self

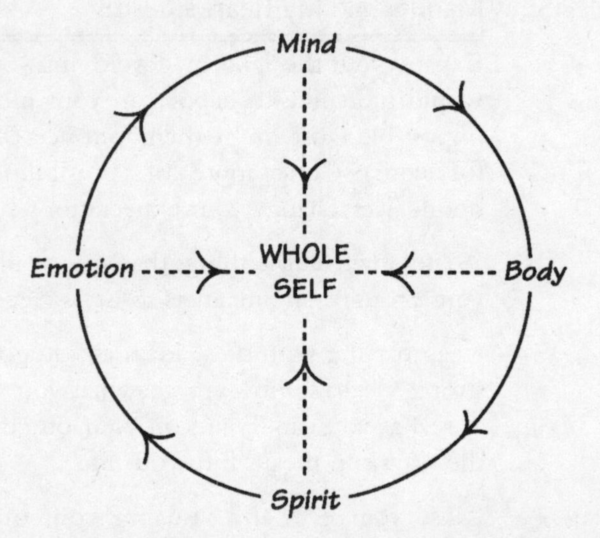

Your own healing rests ultimately with you. Only you can know the delicate interplay between your energies; only you know what you need for your own mental, emotional, spiritual and physical health.

Energy blocks arise when we stop listening to our inner messages; when we don't support our true feelings; when we deny our self-worth and stop taking care of ourselves. As very small children we usually feel free enough to express all our needs but as we grow up we begin to 'protect' our vulnerability by erecting defences (which do not protect us). We are conditioned in all sorts of ways by family culture. We take on negative ideas about ourselves and the world and believe they are true – but they are not true.

If I have learned to believe that I am no good and worthless then these ideas will have an effect at all levels of my being. If I have learned to be low in self-esteem then I will be afraid to express my emotions appropriately; I will hide my true feelings away and this will have a depressing effect on my whole system. Hidden feelings fester and attract other negative beliefs and disabling feelings. No wonder we get ill.

EXERCISE The Ways That My Thoughts and Feelings Affect My Body

How do your thoughts and feelings find physical expression?

1 Think of a time when you were afraid. Recreate the situation as clearly as possible. Feel your fear and check your bodily reactions. How did your body respond?

____

____

____

____

2 Now think of a time when you were very happy. Visualize the scene and re-experience your bodily reactions. How did your body respond? How were your energy levels?

____

____

____

____

3 Remember a time when you were very unhappy. How did your body react?

____

____

____

____

4 Can you remember a time when you were low in self-esteem? Try to get right into the skin of your feelings. What did your body feel like? How was your posture? How was your energy? Did you have any physical symptoms?

____

____

____

____

We all react differently, so take some time to think about the way your own body reacts to different emotional states. Can you see a link between low self-esteem and uncomfortable physical symptoms? Is there a connection between your emotional highs and lows and your physical well-being?

EXERCISE **Body Checks**

Run some body checks throughout the day. When you become aware of your own changes in mood, check how your body reacts. This exercise can be very revealing. As you get more used to 'witnessing' yourself in this way you will begin to become aware of your own body language. Your body talks to you in many different ways, listen to it and respond to its needs.

Our bodies are a reflection of our inner states. What sort of beliefs have created your mental patterns? Are they supportive and nurturing or negative and depressing? Are your emotions allowed expression and release or do they sit inside you attracting angry and resentful thoughts?

Do you want to be healthy? This is an important question to ask yourself. Sometimes there may be 'something in it' for us to be sick. We can use illness as a way to avoid responsibilities and/or we can use our sickness as a way to say no in a situation where we find it difficult to assert ourselves. Perhaps we are low on self-nurturing and our illness means that we will get cared for by someone else.

We cannot cure an illness by 'curing' a physical symptom: that's like putting a plaster over a festering wound. We need to dig deep, beyond our symptoms.

We can learn to change our mental patterns and express our true feelings. When we can support ourselves and recognize our own value; when we are in touch with our emotions and can communicate our needs clearly to other people; when we can take care of our physical needs – then our energy will flow freely and we will experience well-being and a healthy life.

EXERCISE Health and Illness

Are you ready to change your mental patterns? Are you ready to stop being a victim of your own emotions? Do you want to be healthy?

1 Think back to your childhood. What can you remember about your illnesses when you were young?

____

____

____

____

2 What messages did you receive from your parents about being ill?

____

____

____

____

3 How did your parents react to your illnesses?

____

____

____

____

4 Did you enjoy anything about being ill when you were a child?

____

____

____

____

5 Are any of your childhood beliefs about illness affecting your health today?

____

____

____

____

6 In which ways have *you* affected your state of health?

____

____

____

____

7 Do you want to change your condition? What would you like to change?

____

____

____

____

Changing Your Patterns and Healing Yourself

As soon as we begin to trust our intuition and start to care for and nurture ourselves we will increase our self-esteem. Once we respect ourselves we find it easier to be assertive and to communicate our needs to the people in our life. When we are saying what we mean, our body responds to that emotional honesty and our limiting behaviour patterns will start to change. Whenever you are ill, your body is trying to tell you something. Rest and listen to its messages. Why are you ill? Remember that 'thoughts are things': what sort of health are your thought magnets attracting to you? What are your symptoms saying about your energy patterns? Change these patterns to free your energy and start to heal yourself.

We can heal ourselves once we can recognize the probable thought patterns which may correspond to specific illnesses. We can describe each illness in terms of a repeating negative thought pattern and then introduce a healing affirmation which can help to change this pattern.

This way of looking at illness is very empowering; it returns the responsibility for our well-being back to us and so it enhances our self-esteem.

Some Common Ailments, Underlying Thought Patterns and Healing Affirmations

Symptom	Thought Pattern	Healing Affirmation
Back pain	Lack of support, a feeling of having to support others.	*'The universe supports us all.'*
Headaches	Low self-esteem. Criticism of self: 'I am worthless.'	*'I love and value myself.'*
Eye problems	Disliking what you see in your own life.	*'I create what I love to see.'*
Foot problems	Afraid to step forward in life.	*'I move forward easily with love and joy.'*
Neck problems	Inflexibility. Will not see the other side of the story.	*'I can see all sides of an issue. It is safe to be flexible.'*
Throat problems	Reluctance to communicate your needs and fear of change.	*'I can speak up for myself and I am ready to change.'*

Physical symptoms demonstrate energy blocks. Change your thought patterns by making healing affirmations to release these blocks.

The secret of good health is simple:

Love yourself.
Forgive yourself.
Release all blame.
Release all negative thought patterns.
Express your needs.
Take care of your body.
Trust your intuition.
Develop your self-esteem.

You are a valuable and worthy person who deserves to be healthy.

AFFIRMATION 'I deserve perfect health.'

▸ Write this affirmation here:

____

Believe this to be true and heal your life.

Some Positive Affirmations for Health

Make any of these affirmations as often as you can. Write them, say them, sing them. Surround yourself with healing consciousness and feel your energy respond.

'I deserve vibrant health.'
'I love my body.'
'I can heal myself.'
'I listen and respond to my body's messages.'
'I create harmony and balance within my body.'
'The universal life force flows easily through me.'
'I trust my inner messages.'
'It is safe to be well.'
'I am ready to be well, now.'
'I love and value myself.'

For a comprehensive list of illnesses, corresponding thought patterns and healing affirmations see Louise Hay's amazing book, *You Can Heal Your Life.*

11

Discovering Your Life's Work

You are the one and only you. Only you can make the contribution you came here to make. Your combination of special talents is unique and irreplaceable. You have come for a special purpose: to fulfil your life's work.

Do you believe this to be true? Have you discovered your life's work?

What is Your Life's Work?

Doing your life's work is really another way of saying that you are on your own path. The feelings that accompany fulfilling your life's purpose include: 'aliveness', energy, high self-esteem, harmony, interest, enjoyment and satisfaction. If your life feels like this, if what you are doing feels just right, if you are motivated to act in certain ways and you find the energy to do so, then you have found your path. Does your life feel like this?

Your life's work is any activity which energizes you and interests you in this way. It may involve the job you do to earn money; it may not. For example, your life's work now may be to take care of your family. If this brings you satisfaction then this is exactly right for you at the moment. Your path changes character frequently; it may change direction. Perhaps at some point you may feel that the members of your family can begin to look after themselves and you can put some of your energy elsewhere.

You will always know when you are not doing your life's work. You will feel dissatisfied, incomplete, low in self-esteem, low in energy and generally out of sorts. This feeling indicates that it is time to change direction. How do we know in which direction to go?

Think of any of your activities which interest you and give you pleasure. These include all the things that you enjoy and feel confident doing. They may be hobbies, domestic work, writing, caring, mechanical repairs, cooking, driving, fishing, sewing, playing a sport, gardening, painting, playing music . . . the possibilities are endless.

EXERCISE The Things I Most Like to Do

Make a note of your favourite activities and say something about why you enjoy them and what particular aspects give you satisfaction. Dig deep: you may be surprised by your answers.

Activity	Why I enjoy it

These activities are a clue to your life's work. The combination of skills you are using in performing them encompasses your own special brand of talents and strengths, the seeds of your life's work.

Someone who did this exercise included among her chosen activities: reading, knitting, embroidery and looking after her young child. She felt that the exercise had not helped her in any way because she didn't want to make a career of any of these things. However, when we looked at why she enjoyed these activities, the exercise revealed her love of any task which required patience and commitment to a project. She loved taking care of her child but said she wouldn't want to look after other people's children. Two years later this lady is happily working part time in a home for the elderly and is continuing her education by taking 'A' levels at the local college. She is delighted with the developments in her life and is steadily working towards a qualification in the caring professions.

Look behind your answers; try to find the particular skill which you need for each activity and you may discover important links between the most diverse of interests.

Spend more time doing the things you most enjoy. This might mean that you need to become more efficient in the other areas of your life so that you can free up more time to do the things you love. As you do this you are sending an important message to yourself and to the others around you: you are saying that you deserve to do what you most enjoy and that you are prepared to put some effort into making time to do these things.

Sometimes when we start to give our own needs some priority we may encounter resistance from those around us. If you are happy with what you are doing then other people will come to terms with any necessary changes. Remember, no one can make you feel guilty, no one can make you feel anything. You choose to feel your feelings. Beware of using your guilt to stop your progression.

AFFIRMATION

'I am ready to discover my life's work.'

- Write this affirmation here and so declare your decision to find fulfilment in your life.

Turning Your Interests into Your Work

It is possible to turn what you most love to do into a money-making activity: your life's work can become the way you earn your money. Start slowly to make the link between your services and money.

Maybe you like looking after children: start charging for your services. If you are good at repairing things then don't give all your time away for nothing. Sometimes it's nice to use our skills to help people, but if we continue to be forever assisting people in this way, the joy can leave the experience. You might be good at listening to people's problems and you may feel that you would like to help them. This may lead you to thinking about developing your skill, perhaps by taking a counselling qualification in order to turn your aptitude into your work. If you are good at a craft, or painting or writing, maybe you could take that first step towards selling your work. If you never charge for your services then you will need to earn your keep by doing something other than what you like doing best and so you might not have enough time to develop your talents.

Look back to your list of the activities you enjoy the best. Are there any ways in which you could further develop your skills? This doesn't mean dropping all your activities to follow a dream. Rather it means pursuing a dream in a constructive and responsible way. If you need further training or a qualification, then continue your usual affairs and take an evening class or do a correspondence course.

If you are pursuing an ambition then you will find the energy for all these things; interest is a great motivator, boredom is a great depressor. When we are doing what interests us we are affirming our choice of activity; we are saying, 'I deserve to do what I enjoy.' This message increases our self-esteem.

When we are only doing the tasks that don't interest us we are saying, 'I don't deserve to enjoy my life,' and our self-esteem will be very low.

If your dreams seem very far away and you don't know which steps to take, take heart. If you are truly committed to your endeavour, anything is possible. Make sure that your outcome is not 'impossible' because you are afraid to take the steps you might need to take. Sometimes we say, 'Oh, if only I could . . .' or 'I'd love to do/be . . . but it's impossible.' We sometimes make our wishes into pipe dreams because we are afraid to risk failure. If you aren't quite ready at the moment for the work you need to do to bring your dreams into realization, it doesn't matter. When the time is right for you, you will act.

Let's just see what your perfect job would be like. Suspend any limiting beliefs and just create in your imagination the specific qualities that you would like your job to have. At one level we can view this exercise as pure fantasy with no foothold in reality. On the other hand it is as well to remember the power of thought and visualization. By affirming and visualizing a scenario we can bring it into our reality. As you visualize your perfect job try to be specific about as many details as possible. Really see your fantasies in action and picture yourself in the scene. See yourself smiling and confident, really enjoying yourself. The clearer and the more focused your pictures, the stronger your mental magnets become. Send out strong, specific and vibrant images. Use your imagination. Magnetize your new reality.

The following exercise will help you to structure your thoughts so that you can create a strong visualization.

EXERCISE My Perfect Job

Answer the following questions as imaginatively as possible. Remember to suspend any thoughts which limit your style. There are no limitations in this exercise; think as big as you like.

The questions suppose that you are actually doing the job, so answer as if you are.

1 Describe the activities and skills that you are using.

____

2 Do you work indoors or outdoors? Do you travel to work? If so how do you travel? Are you in a town or in the country? Describe your working environment.

3 What is your role? Do you work for a big company, for yourself, as part of a team, or on your own?

4 Describe your working conditions. Is your job high-powered or do you work in a relaxed atmosphere?

5 If you work with other people describe what they are like. What sort of relationships do you have with them?

As you begin to specify your working conditions in this way you will begin to attract all sorts of new possibilities into your life. The changes might not be exactly as you imagine them and these things will not happen overnight but continue with your visualization and slowly but surely, one step at a time, the change will come.

Action Planning

Before we can ever take any action we must first clarify our *intention*, then we can make a *decision* about what we are going to do and then we can *act*. If we have made a strong intention to discover our life's work and we have made some decisions about what we want to happen, we can then take some action.

Action does not just entail going out and making something happen. This of course will be part of the plan, what I call the *outer plan*, but there must also be an *inner plan*. Outer changes are a reflection of inner changes and so I would like to offer the following visualization as a very powerful *inner action plan* for attracting the outer changes that we desire.

VISUALIZATION

Attracting Your Life's Work – An Inner Action Plan

Sit very quietly, relax and close your eyes.

Imagine that your life's work can be represented by a symbol. Visualize what that symbol would be, take the first thing that comes to mind even if it seems inappropriate.

Hold your symbol close to your body and feel its energy filling your whole being . . . hold your symbol like this for a few minutes . . . Sense the energy entering every cell of your body.

There is a hill ahead of you. Carry your symbol to the top of the hill. The journey is very easy for you to accomplish; your symbol is very light to carry. When you reach the top of the hill you see an arched gateway. As you stand under this archway you look behind and see, there below, everything that is a part of your life: all the hopes and fears, loves and disappointments, people and places – all the experiences it took for you to reach where you are today. You feel thankful for *all* your past experiences. The gateway leads to your future, and as you step through, you will throw your symbol high into the air and it will fly out into the world which is your future. Take a few moments to centre yourself before you step through this gateway. Look back at your past again if you wish to. Step through the gateway and release your symbol – this is your future.

This is a powerful visualization which will help you to attract all that you need to discover and to fulfil your life's purpose. The concentrated energy which symbolizes your life's work is spinning through the universe, and it is a strong magnet.

This thought magnet will attract to itself the ways and means for you to actualize your wishes. The answers will not necessarily come in the ways you most expect: be prepared to be flexible and creative in your pursuit of your goal.

From Dream to Reality – An Outer Action Plan

As you move from your intention towards your objective you might find it helpful to structure your thoughts by using the action plan in the table on page 126.

Intention: State one of your objectives.

I want to:____

Method: Decide what steps you will need to take. Try to put them in the order that they need to be dealt with. This might take some thinking about.

Needs: List all the resources that you will need. These may include: help, advice, finance, family support, premises. . . Your initial list may change as time passes and conditions change.

Review: Try to give yourself some realistic deadlines. Decide on certain dates when you will look at your progress and see how you are doing.

Any changes: This is your flexibility column. Your plan needs to have inbuilt flexibility so that you can respond to changes in a creative way instead of being floored if things don't go the way you planned. Any entries here will affect the rest of your plan, so be prepared to make continual changes in your written action plan.

The explanation of this plan sounds so much more complicated than it actually is. Just remember that it is *your* plan and there are no right and wrong ways to go about it. You might need to copy the plan onto another piece of paper, especially if you have a number of objectives. You can use this structure to help you to pursue any goals whether they are short, medium or long term. Use this plan so that it works for you. By the time you reach your objective you may find that your plan is redundant – its work is done. At this stage it may be time to write a new plan so that you can accomplish your next objective.

FROM DREAM TO REALITY – AN OUTER ACTION PLAN				
Intention	**Method**	**Needs**	**Review**	**Any changes**
State an objective	List the steps you need to take	List the resources you will need	Decide a date to review progress	Note any changes that are needed

If your objective seems a bit far-fetched ('I want to be a film star') you could start a little closer to home and join a local drama group or apply to stage school. Everything happens just one step at a time. We can only take the step which is directly in front of us and until we have taken that step we will not be equipped for the next. If your objective seems very far away, just take the step you need to take right now. Use your inner action plan, work on your outer action plan, believe in your goal.

As someone once said, *life is no dress rehearsal.* This is it! This is your life, your gift, your chance to fulfil your life plan. Take that leap of faith; take those risks; there is nothing to fear except fear itself. Follow your star and discover your life's work.

CONCLUSION

Maintaining Your New Levels of Self-Esteem

'Now I'll give *you* something to believe. I'm just one hundred and one, five months and a day'

'I can't believe *that*!' said Alice.

'Can't you?' the Queen said in a pitying tone. 'Try again: draw a long breath, and shut your eyes.'

Alice laughed. 'There's no use trying,' she said: 'One *can't* believe in impossible things.'

'I daresay you haven't had much practice,' said the Queen. 'When I was your age, I always did it for half an hour a day. Why, sometimes I've believed as many as six impossible things before breakfast.'

Lewis Carroll, Alice Through the Looking Glass

Your self-esteem is built upon your self-belief and throughout this book we have been developing techniques to increase our belief in ourselves. I know that sometimes it must have felt as though I was asking you to believe in 'impossible' things. When we are feeling very low it is hard to remember that we are special, worthy and lovable. But it is always true. *You are always special, worthy and lovable.* It is at these times, when the going is hard, that we most need to believe in ourselves. Belief is strong magic.

Throughout this workbook you have used many different methods to help you to increase your self-esteem in all areas of your life. At the root of each of these techniques is one simple message:

Learn to love yourself.

If this sometimes feels like an 'impossible' task then *practise* it. Practise believing that you are wonderful, amazing, deserving, significant – because you are.

Create your own list of affirming self-beliefs. Keep these affirmations in the present tense; keep them positive and practise saying them, *all the time.* Refer to this list immediately you feel your self-esteem falling. Use the examples overleaf if you wish and create some more of your own.

EXAMPLES

'I love and value myself.'

'I am a wonderful and creative person.'

'I deserve the best in life.'

My List of Positive Affirmations

1 ____________________

2 ____________________

3 ____________________

4 ____________________

5 ____________________

6 ____________________

7 ____________________

8 ____________________

9 ____________________

10 ____________________

11 ____________________

12 ____________________

13 ____________________

14 ____________________

15 ____________________

Let this list always be your first resource whenever you start to feel low. Say these things to yourself and they will lift your energy and begin a process which will remind you of your own intrinsic worthiness.

Maintenance Work

You may have read this book and practised the techniques, but you will always need to do what I call your maintenance work. You will *always* be working on your self-esteem because it reflects your own relationship with yourself and that is always changing and developing. Any method which helps you to increase and maintain your levels of self-esteem will be based on the concept of self-nurturing. As soon as we begin to nurture ourselves we sow the seeds of self-esteem. If we feel depressed, unworthy, unlovable, rejected, critical and low in any way, the first steps to recovery always begin with our decision to start to take care of ourselves.

Figure 10 shows a whole range of self-nurturing techniques, all of which we have looked at in the workbook. Whenever you need to lift your energy and start the process of healing yourself of your doubts and fears, just choose any one of these activities and do it. Everyone will be drawn to different techniques; choose the ones that you enjoy the most. Enjoyment is another key to self-esteem.

Figure 10
Self-nurturing activities

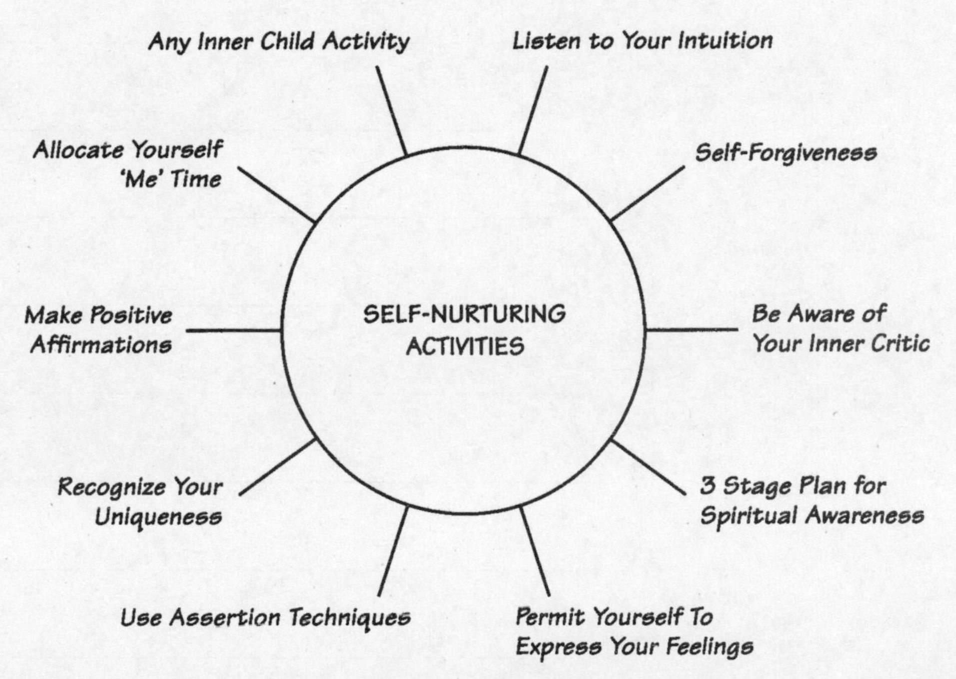

Appreciation

If you are low, then find something to appreciate, however small it may be. However depressed you feel there will always be something that you can appreciate. Find it! When all is bleak and your life has lost its zing, make an appreciation list. You might have to search hard but I promise you it will be worth it. The act of appreciation waters your seeds of self-esteem.

My Appreciation List

I (your name) ________ appreciate ______________________________

I __________________ appreciate ______________________________

I __________________ appreciate ______________________________

I __________________ appreciate ______________________________

I __________________ appreciate ______________________________

Checking Your Levels of Self-Esteem

Scale of Feelings

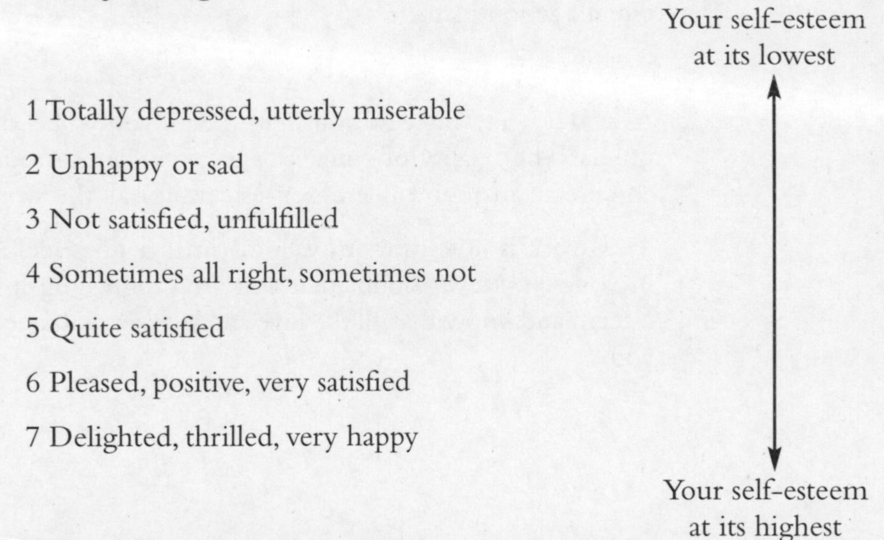

This scale of feelings from 1 to 7 represents the range of emotions from your lowest levels of self-esteem to your highest. Check your self-esteem levels in all areas of your life by filling in the Self-Esteem Progress Chart on page 133. Put a dot in each of the appropriate columns and connect the dots vertically. Use a coloured pencil and make a note of the date you used it in the Colour Key below When you chart your levels again use another colour and then you can compare your self-esteem levels at different times.

	COLOUR KEY
Date	**Colour**

After you have used the chart a few times you will see the peaks and troughs that occur in the different areas of your life. This chart will help you to see which areas you need to work on. You will then be able to go back into the workbook and find the specific techniques that you will need to increase your self-esteem in these particular areas. Develop your own personal self-esteem action plan.

As you learn to increase your self-esteem you will also enhance the lives of others. The quality of your life affects everyone around you, so go ahead and create an abundance of self-esteem for all the world to share.

This work is not always easy. Sometimes it does feel impossible to believe in yourself. Never doubt that you are progressing in your quest for self-esteem and know that all the love and support you need will always be with you.

SELF-ESTEEM PROGRESS CHART							
	1	2	3	4	5	6	7
Partnership, marriage							
Friendships							
Family relationships							
Creative pursuits							
Work, job, main occupation							
General health							
Fitness, physical activities							
Financial situation							
Levels of resistance to victimization							
Freedom of emotional expression							
Ambitions, goals, outcomes							
Trust in own intuition							
The way your time is balanced							
Levels of self-awareness							
Quantity of 'me' time							
Quality of 'me' time							
Ability to be forgiving							
Enjoyment of sensual pleasures							
Enjoyment of fun activities							
Levels of success, recognition							

SUGGESTED FURTHER READING

Bradshaw, John, *Homecoming*, Piatkus, 1991

Gawain, Shakti, *Living In The Light,* Eden Grove Editions, 1988

Gawain, Shakti, *Creative Visualization,* Bantam Books, 1987

Field, Lynda, *Creating Self-Esteem,* Vermilion, 2001

Hay, Louise L, *You Can Heal Your Life,* Eden Grove Editions, 1988

Hay, Louise L, *Love Yourself, Heal Your Life Workbook*, Eden Grove Editions, 1990

Roman, Sanaya, *Personal Power Through Awareness,* H.J. Kramer Inc, 1986

Roman, Sanaya, *Spiritual Growth,* H. J. Kramer Inc, 1989

Roman, Sanaya and Duane Packer, *Creating Money,* H.J. Kramer Inc, 1988

Stone, Hal, PhD and Winkleman, Sidra, PhD, *Embracing Our Selves,* New World Library, 1989

Whitfield, Charles L, MD, *Boundaries and Relationships,* Health Communications Inc, 1993

INDEX